DISRUPTIVE INNOVATION:
STRATEGIES FOR ENTERPRISE GROWTH

DISRUPTIVE INNOVATION: STRATEGIES FOR ENTERPRISE GROWTH

by

Jayanta Bhattacharya

Viva Books Private Limited

New Delhi • Mumbai • Chennai • Kolkata • Bangalore • Hyderabad

First Published 2005

VIVA BOOKS PRIVATE LIMITED

- 4262/3, Ansari Road, Daryaganj, New Delhi 110 002
  Tel 23258325, 23279280 E-mail: vivadelhi@vivagroupindia.net
- 215-216 New Apollo Estate, 2nd Floor, Mogra Lane, Andheri (E), Mumbai 400 069
  Tel 56997844, 56997845 E-mail: vivamumbai@vivagroupindia.net
- Jamals Fazal Chambers, 26 Greams Road, Chennai 600 006
  Tel 28294241, 28290304 E-mail: vivachennai@vivagroupindia.net
- B-103, Jindal Towers, 21/1A/3 Darga Road, Kolkata 700 017
  Tel 22816713 E-mail: vivakolkata@vivagroupindia.net
- 7, GF, Sovereign Park Aptts., 56-58, K. R. Road, Basavanagudi, Bangalore 560 004
  Tel 26607409 E-mail: vivabangalore@vivagroupindia.net
- 101-102, Moghal Marc Apartments, 3-4-637 to 641, Narayanguda,
  Hyderabad 500 029 Tel 27564481
  E-mail: vivahyderabad@vivagroupindia.net

ISBN 81-309-0187-0

Published by Vinod Vasishtha for Viva Books Private Limited,
4262/3 Ansari Road, Daryaganj, New Delhi 110 002.

Printed & bound by Raj Press, R-3 Inderpuri, New Delhi - 110 012.

DEDICATION

Dedicated to the enduring and loving memory
of my late Grandmother Srimati Shishirkana Bhattacharya.

CONTENTS

PREFACE

In the continuum of technology development and the related market it is always observed that continuity favours the embedded and entrenched interests that inhibit market growth. Disruption in the continuum creates more opportunities in the market both for the established players of the business as well as for the new entrants. For example, the bank ATMs have disrupted the traditional manual tellers in the bank and have expanded opportunities by means of increased access to capital. The examples galore around us – typewriters giving way to desk tops, mainframe computers sharing the market with the PCs, text messaging in the cell phones are giving way to the video images, and expensive detergent brands are making room for affordable brands for greater population. The radical and disruptive innovation will continue to change our lives, whether or not we are ready to accept them. It is proving increasingly fatal for the firms to ignore them, and also for the individuals to shy away from the opportunities they can create.

Research shows that such disruptions can be understood, anticipated, tracked, managed and can even be encouraged with in the organization. A firm can map its pathways before, to avert the disruption and even can take the disruption created opportunity.

To know how you and your organization can take the opportunities from such disruptions, read the analysis, 12 detailed case studies, numerous case examples and references given for easy-paced reading. This book is a must for managers, students and academics of business and technology development and also for the general reader.

You have heard about and read Clayton Christensen, Gary Hamel, Clark Gilbert, Michael Porter, Bruee Vojak and many others speaking on disruptive innovations but might not have read them together in coherent analyses. This book attempts to do just that.

Disruption Lexicon

Asymmetries	Skills, processes, talents, assets or outputs an organization possesses or produces that its competitors do not and cannot copy at a cost that affords economic rents. They are rare, inimitable, and non substitutable.
Disruption and disruptive	Disruption is a break or stop in the continuous process. "Disruptive" is the capability of an entity (firm or organization) to be able to cause disruption.
Incumbent	Existing and entrenched player of the market; established and mature firm; firm playing by the rules (some, or all set by it) of the market.
Invention and innovation	Invention refers to the discovery of new methods or materials, that is, to the discovery of new knowledge. Innovation refers to attempts to commercialize an invention.
Resources	Asymmetries that produce superior economic returns: examples include technical skills, patents, scarce raw materials sources, exclusive alliances and A-one reputation.
Capabilities	Resources can be configured into capabilities—bundles of complementary resources such as tacit knowledge, administrative skills, routines, and physical assets with the flexibility to generate adaptive and valuable outputs. Today capability is being used in place of competence because capability tends to add competence with technology and products on skills.

Core capabilities	Capabilities especially central to competitive advantage that form the basis for the strategic development of the firm. These can often be leveraged across different products and markets, and typically comprise or orchestrate other capabilities.
Organization design	How a firm allocates, controls, and motivates its resources. Formal aspects include policies and priorities, structure (authority, role, and task definitions, accountability, liaison devices) and information, human resources, and planning systems. Informal aspects include firm culture (values, beliefs, styles of interaction) and communication networks.
Capability configuration	System of reinforcing elements incorporating core capabilities and the organizational designs in which they are embedded, and that renew, adapt and support these capabilities.
Road map	An extended look at the future of a chosen field of inquiry composed from the collective knowledge of the brightest drivers of change in the field.
Technology	Technology refers to the theoretical and practical knowledge, skills and artifacts that can be used to develop products and services as well as their production and delivery systems.
Technology roadmapping	Technology roadmapping is a needs-driven technology planning process to help identify, select and develop technology alternatives to satisfy a set of product needs. It brings together a team of experts to develop a framework for

	organizing and presenting the critical technology-planning information to make the appropriate technology investment decisions and to leverage those investments.

Disruption Lexicon (Miller, 2003; Walsh, 2004; Hill and Rothaermel, 2003; Bhattacharya, 2004)

INTRODUCTION

Why do our life-style patterns change? Have you ever wondered how life was before we began to use computers? Small daily innovation bring a continuum of change.

There are plenty of innovations. Some are simple changes around us on our concepts to things, procedures and behaviours. For instance, Pentium 4 would be considered an improvement over the preceding types; flexi-time work today allows employees more choices and provides more opportunities for work-life balance; and generous after-sales service is definitely better than a hasty goodbye to a client. So innovation leads to two things : change, and famously called by Schumpeter in 1934 as "Creative Destruction".

Innovation is the process of successful commercial exploitation of a technical invention backed by a theoretical concept. Innovations are not uncommon in an organization. In fact, in daily routines many employees try to do some things every day differently from what they did yesterday, to derive some financial benefit for the organization. Also every organization with the help of in-house Research and Development (R&D) tries to improve the product quality with some innovation. One such example is very visible: almost all toothpaste manufacturers in addition to the brand of toothpaste for general use also gradually bring out some toothpastes for specific use like gum care, cavity protection, and with mouth freshener by means of some small innovations. All these are incremental innovations that exploit the present and briefly-expanded market. They are continuous in nature. The continuous innovations generally target niche market. Some innovations, however, are more dramatic and probably more complex than the rest. These are disruptive innovations. As the term implies, they do have the power to alter the chain of events and change our lives radically. The atomic bomb over Hiroshima did alter the chain of events in World War II and the art of war was never the same again. Consider the invention of the light bulb, radio, television, contact lenses, automobile, airplane, organ transplants, genetics and the high profile mobile phones and texting. We are unable to imagine how life was and will be without them! The last one, of course, disrupted the cue for landlines. George Por (2003) listed four critical attributes of disruptive innovations: they are mission-critical in that they revolutionize the business; they represent breakthroughs; they are often products of interdisciplinary collaboration; and they not only question "what" and "how" but also the "why".

An idea is called disruptive if it meets one or more of the three tests (Hamel and Getz, 2004).

* It changes customer expectations and behaviours. For example, Bank ATMS have changed the way people use their money.
* It changes the basis of competitive advantage. The proliferation of digital cameras, for instance, has altered the basis for competition in the photographic film industry.
* It changes industry economics. For example, with its simplified route structure, no-frills service and flexible work practices, Air Deccan can dramatically change the traditional cost structure for airlines.

In a similar vein, Thomond and Lettice (2002) advanced several characteristics of a disruptive innovation: 1. It is able to meet unfulfilled needs of an emerging niche or market. 2. While highly rated by the niche market, its performance attributes are not initially appreciated by the mainstream. 3. Niche market adoption enables investment that in turn increases performance. 4. Awareness and increasing evidence of performance influence changes in the mainstream market in favour of the innovation. 5. The change in the mainstream market's perceptions enables the innovation to disrupt and replace the existing mainstream product.

The introduction of disposable diapers addressed to mothers of young children showed disruption capability. The early adopters saw the "smartness" of the shift because of two obvious benefits:

more time at the users' disposal considering that they were freed from laundry and ease of use even during rainy days. Laundry savings served to offset the costs of one-time use. These eventually "pulled" the rest of the market to adopt and disrupted the use of re-usable (cloth) diapers. Of course, design and use have now been extended to adults. Table-1 describes the examples of succuessful disruptive innovation.

Table 1: Examples of Successful Disruptive Innovation

PROCESS	
Before	After
Cement Retailing	Concrete Retailing
Traditional Retailing Brokers	Online Brokers
Inspection Quality Control	Vendor-managed Quality Control
PRODUCT	
Before	After
VHS	DVD
Mini Computers & mainframes	Personal Computers
Cathode Ray Tubes	Transistors
SERVICE	
Before	After
Bank Teller	Bank ATM
Airline ticket	Total tourism package
Group Travel package	Customised Travel package

UNDERSTANDING AND ENABLING DISRUPTIVE INNOVATION

Innovations can be thought of as falling onto a continuum from evolutionary to revolutionary. While evolutionary innovation is critical to sustaining and enhancing shares of mainstream markets revolutionary breakthroughs lie at the core of wealth creation (Schumpeter 1942). In fact by definition, revolutionary innovations serve as the basis of future technologies, products, services and industries. The term 'disruptive innovation' has been used to describe innovation that is highly revolutionary or discontinuous in nature, in which customers and consumers embrace new paradigms in favour of the old. This term is becoming more widely recognised.

A disruptive innovation not necessarily means leading to a radically new product. Often its usefulness is established in the upper stratum of the market, but its commercial exploitation is yet incomplete.The market appears as if from nowhere with ability to create massive and sustainable sources of wealth. It tends to have its roots in technological discontinuities, such as one that enabled Motorola's rise to prominence with the first generation of cell phones, or in fast-spreading fads like the collector card game Poke'mon. A disruptive innovation brings to market a product not as good as the products in the current market, and so it cannot be sold to the mainstream up-market customers. But it is simple and is more affordable. It takes root in an undemanding portion of the market, then improves from that simple beginning to intercept with the needs of customers in the mainstream later. The table-3 depicts the market scenario in the 4th quadrant for disruptive innovation.

Christensen (2004) argued that a disruptive innovation is not a breakthrough from a technological sense, but instead of sustaining the trajectory of improvement that has been established in a market, it disrupts it and redefines it by bringing to the market something that is simpler.

This book explores the concept of disruptive innovation as presented in the literature and how it differs from other types of innovation.

To begin to understand disruptive innovation it is useful to again consider some examples as given in table-1.

Following the diktats of creative destruction we see the fall of large organizations. For example, Smith Corona, one of the dominant firms in type writer industry, failed to adapt to the arrival of the personal computer and word processing software, and went bankrupt.

Few organisations understand or have established track records for undertaking successful disruptive innovation. In fact most are reluctant to follow this path and find themselves disadvantaged by embedded structures.

Effects of Disruption

The desire to maintain a stable and efficient context to satisfy mainstream market demands, forces many organisations into a focus on the 'familiar', the 'mature' and the 'proximate' business. Thus most organisations fall into learning traps preventing them from 'exploring' potentially disruptive ideas. In addition the problem of typically going by standard business routines actually hinder truly creative thinking. It would appear that the fundamental nature of disruptive innovation necessitates organisations to lead and not follow. Market research, however, can provide little or no benefit for exploring the potential of disruptive ideas, in fact it can even obstruct radical idea development (Christensen, 2000).

If an organisation manages to foster a potentially disruptive idea, not only does it often face huge problems getting internal support but there are massive obstacles to overcome to get it adopted by the mass market. The obstacles faced by companies trying to 'cross the chasm' from early market acceptance to gain the support of the 'early majority' and how to deal with the problems occur when early majority begins to rapidly adopt the new technology or change. Disruptive innovation only begins to be truly realised when the marketplace shifts to adopt a new paradigm in what he calls the "tornado" of adoption. Once the tornado begins it is not long before the majority of potential customers in the marketplace have undergone dramatic change in their past behaviour with the promise of gaining equally dramatic benefits from the new paradigm. Figure-1 explains the phenomena in great detail.

The market adoption of new technology follows the life cycle that is dominated by disruptive innovation that needs support from application and product innovation, to bring about the creation of new market category (table-2).

New paradigms represent discontinuties in trajectories of progress as defined within earlier paradigms – where a technological paradigm is a pattern of solutions for selected technological problems.

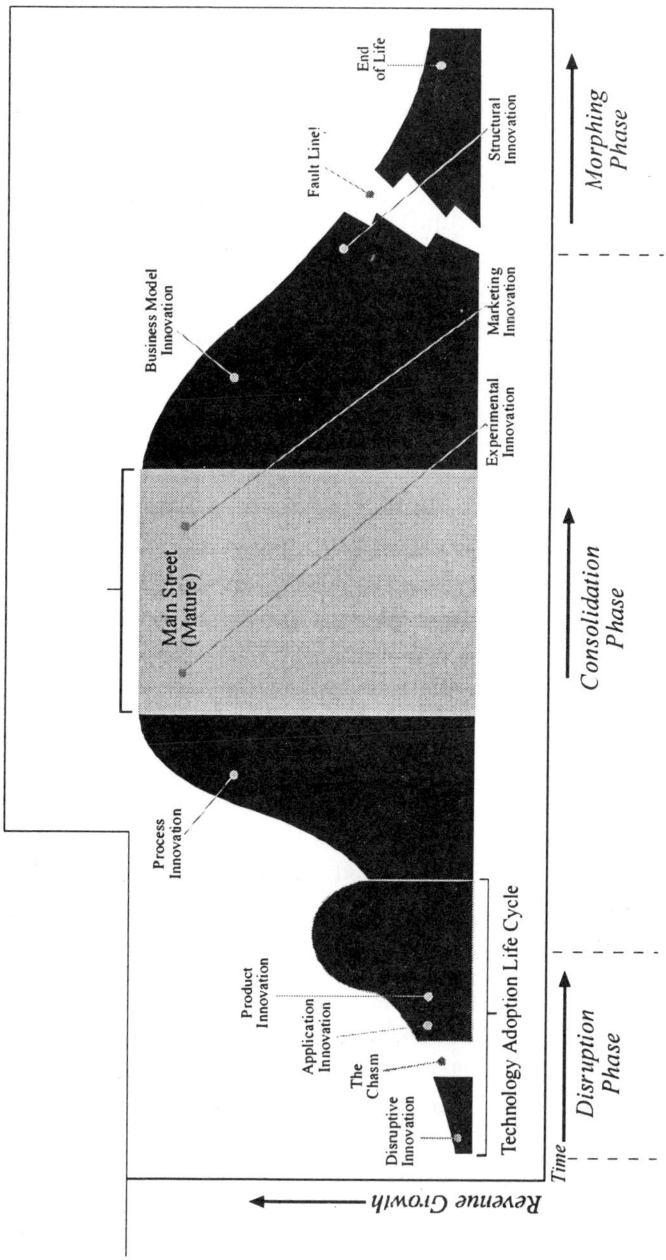

Fig. 1 The market development life cycle for disruptive innovation and its sustainability (please see table. 2 for more details).

In fact, new paradigms redefine the future meaning of progress and a new class of problems becomes the target of normal incremental innovation. Thus for a discontinuous or sudden innovation to be disruptive, successful exploitation is vital, which results in significant transformation of the mainstream market and its value proposition. The internet-driven on-line shopping was a disconutinuous innovation in 1998, could not be successful till 2002, because of poor understanding of the market.

Table 2: The market and Innovation Development Cycle

Market Development phases	Innovation phases	Market Features	Innovation Features	Comments
Early market	Disruptive Innovation	New technology attracts early adopters enthusiasts and visionaries	It tends to have root in technological discontinuities	Pragmatic buyers are curious but make no comments. The press says it is the next big thing.
The Chasm	———	The technology is in the market for some time and has lost novelty, e.g., fuel cells, on-demand computing, of its safe purchase.		It' s acceptance is not widespread convince the pragmatists wireless.

Bowling Alley	Application Innovation	The technology is gaining acceptance in one or more niche market and also in the adjacent niches (hence the bowling pin metaphor). Within each niche there are followers who are ready to pursue long with the technology.	Takes existing technologies in to new market to serve new purposes, as when digital camera being brought in the mobile phones. Onstar took global positioning system into automobile market.	Outside the niche however the technology is largely unknown.
Tornado	Product Innovation	The technology has passed the test of usefulness and is now being perceived as necessary and standard. The benefits are clearly visible and exploitable in business. The pragmatists are the rushing	Takes established offers in market to a next level as when Toyota brings in a new car, or when Intel offers a new processor.	Customers of diverse fields are making their first purchase and many new customers are joining in across the population. The comptetion is fierce at

		in. The example is the basic mobile phones in India today. The growth rates are in double digit.		this satge because large amount of capital by investors is available for picking.
Main Street (Early)	Process Innovation	The era of hyper growth has susbsided but there are few potent areas of growth. A first wave of consolidation and convergence results in market sharing by different entities.	Makes processes for established offers in market more effective or effecient. Introducing the similar mobile phone at much cheaper price by the Korean and Chinese players.	Even companies with small market will do well. This is the time when standardization with result.
Main Street (Mature)	Experimental and Marketing Innovation	Category growth has flattened and commoditization is increasing. The products are visible everywhere. A second wave	Makes superficial modications that improve customer's experience of established products	Customers now take this category for granted and the press know longer talk about it

		of consolidation and convergence will result with market leaders creating top-line growth, both organically as well by alliance and acquisitions	and processes. They are delighters (songs as ring tones), or reassurers (package tracking from FedEx) when packages are insured.	and on the good side there is no obsolecing technology on horizon and so, the market risk even is negligible
Main Street (Declining)	Business Model Innovation	The catagory has lost its sheen and the market dominators are doling out the same variety of by an technology.	Reframes established proposition to the customer or company's established role in the value chain or both. Examples: Gillette's move from rators to razor blades and IBM's shift to on-demand computing. move from rators to razor blades and IBM's	Everybody is apprehen sive about the next generation technology; The situation is ripe for disruption either by an obsolescing technology or a radically innovative business model.

Fault Line And End	Structural Innovation	The technology obsolescence has struck like an earthquarke, exposing the fault line become an what a attractive sells and what the market desires. The next generation tornado is wrecking havoc on installed bases of established vendors.	Capitalizes disruption to restructure industry relationship. Innovating in banking sector by liberalizing rules and procedures for taking loans, ICICI or HDFC has revolutionized the way the people take loan today.	The customers are much less willing to spend. Leveraged between company mechanism for monopolizing the remaining market opportunity.

Thus the evolution of the value networks surrounding emerging or niche markets, that have not been satisfied by existing paradigms, can significantly disrupt and threaten key players in mainstream networks. Such change significantly affects the rise and fall of populations within organisational communities (Astley, 1985). The dissatisfaction over the delay of getting the landlines in India provided a potential market space for disruptive cell-phones.

The extent of disruption that major breakthroughs cause can be broken down into subgroups of 'product' and 'process', furthermore, these can be either 'competence-destroying' or 'competence-enhancing' (Tushman and Anderson,1986). Competence-destroying discontinuities are highly disruptive, requiring new skills, abilities and knowledge, are initiated by new entrants-or spin-off companies (Christensen, 1997; Hamel, 2000). They increase environmental turbulence and market uncertainty, usually delivering a new product class, a significant product substitute or a radical new way of making a product. Alternatively, competence-enhancing discontinuties "represent an order-of-magnitude improvement over prior products, yet build on existing know-how" (Tushman and Anderson, 1986, p.442). They are associated with little or even decreased environmental turbulence and reduced market uncertainty. Thus disruptive innovation occurs in both products and processes and is at the extreme end of the continuum of discontinuous innovation.

Veryzer (1998) showed that organisations could deliver commercial discontinuities and innovations that are both commercially discontinuous with each requiring a different management approach. He showed how customers perceive that value attributes of a product or service are important to discontinuties with potential for disruptive innovation. It has been shown that revolutionary product or service innovation involves the application of significant new technologies or significant new combinations of technologies, to new market opportunities (Tushman and Nadler, 1986), this can be developed through novel technologies and technoogy upgradation.

New Opportunities

Hamel (2000) suggests that the system level is where the real benefits of 'non-linear' or disruptive innovation can be found. He states that organisations can disruptively innovate with products or services but the real value is only unlocked when the larger system is factored into the disruption. By unpacking the 'business model' and exposing it to disruptive thinking. Hamel states that 'Business Concept Innovation' occurs and that this is the real essence of revolutionary innovation, causing disruption to preconceived ideas, markets and entire value networks. This would finally lead to business model innovation, critical for the success of the disruption (see figure - 2).

Thus, revolutionary innovations fall onto a continuum ranging from 'radical incrementalism' - that delivers significant change to the mainstream customer which, is mostly competence enhancing with low environment turbulence and low market uncertainty -to 'disruptive innovations' - that deliver transformational change to the mainstream market and its value attributes which, are mostly competence destroying with high environmental turbulence and high market uncertainty.

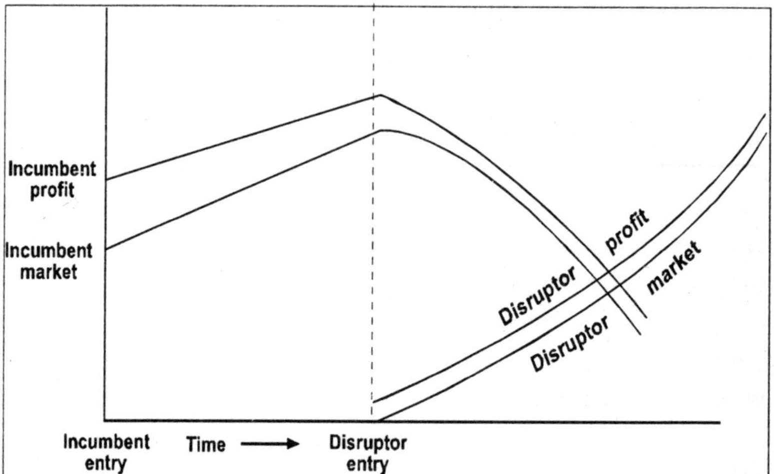

Fig. 2 Effect of Disruption (Note : Saturated market performance is mostly linear but Disruptor market is non-linear).

Does disruption create opportunity only for the new entrant? We will see in the following that it creates opportunities for change, for almost all. Table-3 shows ordinary market scenario where there is scope of disruption.

Table 3: Market Scenario

1 High Value Customer High Quality Product Continuum Linear Market	4 Low Value Customer High Quality Product Non Linear Market Disruption
2 High Value Customer Low Quality Product Unsustaniable Market	3 Low Value Customer Low Quality Product Continuum Linear Market

Here is one pessimist-optimist story. The pessimist says "We die a little everyday". The optimist says "Each day brings us closer to our resurrection". The truth is - life brings us incremental changes with disruptive results. The primary task of successful living is that we learn to transform.

Asymmetry Advantage

When companies have the same capabilities and motivation, they have the necessary skills to fight a disruptive attack.

Asymmetires are the important differences of motivation of skills. Asymmetries of motivation occur when one firm wants to do something that another firm specifically does not want to do, on the other hand asymmetires of skills occur when one firm's strength is another firm's weakness.

Asymmetries allow disruptive attackers to enter a market, grow without incumbent oversight and interference, and mitigate the incumbent's response when it is finally motivated to counterattack. The result of asymmetric battles often is the seemingly sudden end of a great firm. From the incumbent's perspective, every action it takes is rational. Disruption is the strategy that creates and capitalizes on asymmetries of motivation and skills. It naturally follows a three-step process (Christensen, 2004).

Step 1 : Entrants enter behind a shield of asymmetric motivation: early incumbent response leads to flooding.

Incumbents sleep over what in retrospect turn out to be multibillion-dollar opportunities because attackers take advantage of asymmetries of motivation. Disruptive markets start among customers that appear to the incumbent to be either undesirable or nonexistent because they do not see the opportunities. The initial absolute size of a disruptive opportunity is generally too small to justify any substantial amount of investment or even management attention. But the highly motivated see light at the end of the tunnel.

Asymmetric motivation shields disruptive companies from competitive response because their potential challengers are just not interested in fighting. Even if they fight their hearts aren't in it. The battle matters more to their opponents. Remember the old saying "It is not the size of the dog in the fight. It is the size of the fight in the dog."

Gauging asymmetries is so essential to predicting outcomes because the availability of information about a threat or opportunity has little influence on who wins and who loses. What makes the difference is what a company does with that information. Incumbents usually see the same technologies that entrants do. Because of their processes and values, however, incumbents predictably "flood" the technology into the largest and most obvious market applications.

What causes the oversupply? Managers tend to adopt innovations in ways that make sense to their business. They know the markets their companies serve. Those markets appear large and measurable. The companies have established processes to help them penetrate that market. So the established competitors in a market naturally choose to bring all innovations-sustaining and disruptive-to their core markets where their best customers reside.

When an existing firm tries to insert a product or service with disruptive potential into its processes, what comes out from the other end tends not to be disruptive. Instead of embracing the innovative product's inherently disruptive nature, the incumbent inevitably tries to morph the product to fit into its existing processes and values. It alters the innovation to enhance its appeal to core customers and fit within its operating model. The problem with flooding is that it changes the innovation in ways that ignore its inherent disruptive energy. It takes an innovation from a situation in which its unique features are valuable to a situation in which its unique features are a liability.

For example, Kodak first began to sense that digital imaging might pose a threat to its core business in the mid-1990s. It invested more than $2 billion in research and development. However, it framed the challenges as, "How do we make digital imaging good enough to serve as a viable replacement to silver halide film in our core market?" By seeking to create high-priced performance-competitive digital products. Kodak missed much of the disruptive growth driven by inexpensive digital imaging. Kodak eventually established a strong market share after introducing a very low-cost camera, but only after spending $2 billion trying to maximize its cameras' performance.

Flooding explains why so many disruptive innovations originate from within incumbents but are ultimately commercialized by separate organizations. When a firm develops the germ of a disruptive idea, it often falls prey to the temptation to force opportunity to its mainstream market. The momentum behind the widely practiced mantra "serve our customers" is often nearly impossible to overcome. The mainstream market tends to reject the innovation. Frustrated managers and engineers leave form a new company and discover a new market where the innovation has value.

Step 2 : New entrants grow and improve; incumbents despair.

As disruptive attackers follow their own competitive economics of scale and optimum resourcing they make inroads into the low end of the market or begin pulling less demanding customers into a new context of use. What happens when the disruptive entrant enters the market.

Incumbents naturally first dismisses the threat, but soon look for cover or despair. What looks highly attractive to the entrant continues to look relatively unattractive to the incumbent. The asymmetric motivation leads naturally to incumbents abandoning the low end of the existing long-distance market to cell phones. VSNL initially miscalculated in the beginning that the mobile phone market would confine to the rich and salaried customers. But entrants like Airtel and Reliance disrupted the low end market with marketing innovations and registered larger number.

Remember, incumbents focus on of delivering up-market sustaining innovations that allow them to earn premium prices by reaching much flirted customers. They view flight as a positive development. When there are large groups of upperclass customers in the higher tiers of a market, incumbents can beat a long and profitable up-market retreat. The customers incumbents leave behind tend to be the least attractive. Sales can go up (high price points replace low price points). Margins typically go way up. The incumbent stops worrying about disloyal, dissatisfied, low-paying customers whom outsiders may term "distractions" and instead focuses on very loyal highly satisfied, high-paying customers.

How to identify when looking for cover is in progress? Changes in customers or product mix can be a clear sign as are plans to discontinue low-end product lines or to stop servicing old versions of products. Companies tend to announce that they are "focusing on the core" of "seeking higher margin opportunities" when flight is in progress. Sometimes companies will launch diversification efforts to flee from an attacker.

Step 3 : Entrant takes position with asymmetric skills.

The small irritant gets big -too big for an incumbent to ignore. The number of undershot customers dwindles. But when incumbents become cornered, they face two problems. First, asymmetric motivation still stymies effective response. Even though the new opportunity may appear big, it typically requires a different business model. Even worse, incumbents are now at the mercy of asymmetric skills. Disruptive innovations typically introduce new benefits to a market, usually centered on convenience, simplicity, customization, or affordability. As the entrant steadily increases the grip of the market, it builds the ability to do whatever is required to succeed in its context. When the incumbent has retreated into the highest tiers of its market and joins the fight reluctantly because there is no room for further retreat, it is at a competitive disadvantage. As the game changes to the one the disruptor plays best, it is very hard for the incumbents to develop new skills so much quickly.

By the time Bell companies firmly established themselves, they developed unique competencies related to transmitting the human voice over relatively short distances. They established skills in acoustics, network management customers service and so on. Western Union had none of these skills. Its business did not need to solve these problems. It was on the wrong side of asymmetries. Western Union couldn't suddenly become a viable competitor after the telephone had been improving for twenty-five years. Similarly, Digital Equipment Corporation couldn't match the flexibility of the personal computer assemblers' processes, Sears couldn't match the inventory turns and low prices of the discount retailers and so on.

Overdependence on Strength Is Weakness

It is expected that the firms will begin with small but inimitable strengths, and build them into powerful resources, much in the manner the core competence, or more appropriately today, dynamic competencies. There are other more surprising paths a firm can take. Firms will build on valuable resources or capabilities, which will tend to be rare but on asymmetries that can be explained as, "Inimitable differences between themselves and other firms that in their initial states could in no way be considered valuable". The asymmetries will manifest themselves in the form of teams, projects, contacts, knowledge or even business units that will be truly distinctive and could not be imitated by others at a cost that would also provide economic returns.

In disruptive circumstances, entrants win because they arc - often unknowingly - taking advantage of the asymmetries on their side. An incumbent's strengths are its weaknesses. Its values, which make sure it delivers excellent products to demanding customers, stop it from going after markets where ultimately its strongest competitors will forge their processes and values. The incumbent's processes, those that allow it to serve its customers well, are weaknesses when the game changes and new capabilities are necessary. Fleeing from the disruptive attacker feels good in the short term but further deprives the incumbent of the necessary skills to compete. The end can come swiftly and can appear stunning to the untrained eye. Typically, the best an incumbent can do is to belatedly acquire the winning firm and stave off ultimate destruction.

In sustaining circumstances, incumbents win because they are the ones attacking with asymmetries on their side. Consider an entrant that tries to bring a radical sustaining innovation to an incumbent's best customers.

There are no asymmetric motivations here. Incumbents are very motivated to go after this market. The incumbent's processes are relative strengths, not relative weaknesses. A new firm that attempts to introduce a radical sustaining innovation almost guarantees itself a long, bruising fight. Unless the new firms sell their advanced product quickly to the established leaders or have extremely patient, deep-pocketed investors, incumbents will spend more, produce better products and services, and ultimately force the entrants out of the market. There is always, however, scope to fight back.

There are three factors that contribute to asymmetric motivation, all of which relate to firm values. The first factor relates to an opportunity's absolute size. An opportunity that looks interesting and large to a small firm might look uninteresting and small to a big firm. To the emerging telephony companies, the emerging local communications market looked boundless. Through the lenses of VSNL, the cellphone market initially looked inconsequential. Similarly, a meaningful growth opportunity for a Fortune 50 company will be very different than that of a start-up. The second factor relates to an opportunity's initial customer. Disruptive markets start among customers that appear to the incumbent to be either undesirable or nonexistent. Entrants are motivated to serve the new market. The final factor relates to an opportunity's business model. Disruptive entrants use business models that do not fit the ways established firms make money. Gross margin per unit sold tends to be lower but turnover or asset utilization tends to be higher Disruptive innovations tend to be off-the-shelf products, in which the customer turns either to a group of specialist firms or to themselves to provide postsales service. A company that has a business model based on long-term relationships and multi-year support agreements will have little interest in selling a product that diminishes those revenue streams. In Fig 2 Asymmetric Motivation shows the effect of disruption in the market.

How can one observe asymmetric motivation in action? When companies take completely different actions that make sense to both of them, it is a sign that there are asymmetries. When one firm calls an industry "unprofitable" while another firm calls that market "important," asymmetries are at work. For example, in the 1990s. Cisco raced to capture more of the networking equipment market while IBM sought to leave networking equipment to focus on higher-margin services. On the other hand, when an incumbent announces an entrant's emergent growth market is a strategic priority, it could indicate a lack of asymmetries.

Asymmetric skills act as a weapon a company can brandish to attack its opponents. Remember, a company's skills come largely from its processes. A process comes from repeatedly solving a particular class of problem. Processes are designed to get the same thing done, over and over - and as such they tend to be inflexible. Asymmetric skills arise when one firm, through repeatedly completing the same task, has developed a unique ability to do something that its competitor is uniquely unable to do.

How can you tell if combatants have asymmetric skills? Make a list of the tasks the company has repeatedly addressed, for which formal and informal processes have gelled. Compare the list to the nature of tasks required to succeed in the disruptive market. If a company's processes facilitate its doing what it needs to get done in a market context, it has the requisite skills to take that market (Christensen, 1997).

Circumstances in Which High-Potential Disruptive Development Will Prove Disappointing

There are certain situations in which—even though disruptive entrants seem to be on an unencumbered trajectory toward success—incumbents still emerge triumphant (Christensen, 1997).

Understanding asymmetries allows us to identify two specific circumstances in which the disruptive process is likely to come off the rails. The first circumstance occurs when the industry context makes incumbent flight unpalatable. The second occurs when an entrant fails to develop a distinctive business model or to create unique skills in its early stages, making co-option the natural choice for the incumbent. In these circumstances, expect to see tough competitive battles after the aggressive growth phase.

Industry contexts in which incumbent is under threat

Fleeing up-market is only a natural choice for incumbents when there is an adequately sized, attractive market at the high end. This isn't always the case firms might not have the ability to reach the next tier of undershot customers. Or undershot customers might not exist. Or an incumbent's cost structure and business model sometimes prevent it from leading low-end markets (Christensen, 1997).

Think about the battle between AT&T and MCI. MCI grew without real interference from AT&T for a few years. But AT&T eventually had to respond to MCI. AT&T's business model depended on amortizing large fixed costs over a wide number of users. Flight to the high end—which typically entails focusing on smaller numbers of customers who are willing to pay high prices for the most advanced products and services—really wasn't a competitive option. Because AT&T cared about the customers MCI took from it. it ultimately decided to fight back. The resulting "long-distance wars" of the 1980s and 1990s cost both companies millions in advertising, with the "winner" capturing a bigger slice of an increasingly less lucrative market.

When firms can't choose to run away we can expect them to fight. Entrants can no longer hide behind asymmetric motivation. And if this happens early enough, entrants don't have the time to refine their asymmetric skills. The result is often a bruising battle for market share. This concept helps explain the no-win situation facing many players in the aviation industry.

There are myriad market opportunities across which to leverage asymmetries. Just as organizations are complex so are the markets. There are many niches, segments, types of clients, untapped needs, etc. Even in the unlikely event that a firm's asymmetries are few and fixed, they are still good to be some especially appropriate market niches across which the firm can leverage to competitive advantage.

Disruption is not enough!

Incumbents turn back when they have no up-market to penetrate. When else are incumbents strongly motivated to respond to disruptive attackers? When an entrant makes money in similar ways or uses similar processes as the incumbents. An entrant runs into trouble if it does not develop a business model that is unattractive to the incumbent, or if it does not hone unique skills that are matched to the disruptive business It can create initial growth by taking advantage of the incumbent's disinterest in small, immeasurable markets. But once the entrant has proved to the world that the market exists, the incumbent can muster its internal resources to co-opt the innovation, unless the entrant has made that path unattractive or not easily attainable natural incumbent motivation shifts from fret to fight. And in direct fights with comparable motivation to win, the incumbents have some real advantages to bring to the battle (Gilbert and Bower, 2002).

What indicates an attempt at co-option? One sign is an effort by incumbents to develop products or services that mimic the entrant's offering. Acquiring and attempting to integrate one of the class of disruptive entrants is a clear signal that the incumbent is attempting co-option. When business model or process asymmetries don't exist, co-option becomes a viable incumbent response strategy.

Incumbents might still miss much of the growth created by the disruptive innovation, of course, depending on when they initiate following a co-option strategy and where they implement it. Growth-driven co-option needs to occur early and entails going after an entrant's core customers In essence, an incumbent co-opts the disruption by augmenting its existing product and service offerings to appeal to new customers. When confronted with wireless technologies, for example, the incumbent phone companies chose growth-driven co-option. They developed wireless technology using internal resources and tried to market it to new customers.

Defensive co-option usually occurs later in a technology's development. Incumbents recognize that they have lost the game in the volume end of the market and do what they can to block incursions from below. For example. Oracle introduced its disruptive relational database in the minicomputer market in the 1985. When IBM realized that Oracle had decisively won the game in that market, it introduced a relational database at the low end of its mainframe market, attempting to block Oracle's advance. Look in to an effort to target customers and company announcements to see if companies are following growth-driven or defensive strategies. For instance, a company announcing that the disrupter's home market is a strategic priority is a clear signal of a growth-driven response.

Discovering Asymmetries and Related Resources and Capabilities

To do well, firms need to develop important competencies or resources that rivals cannot match firms cannot attain sustainable resources by copying others. They need to look inside. It was only when Shana realized that its inimitable capability was bridging operating systems, not writing forms software rivals could match, that the company was able to develop the most profitable outputs.

Is asymmetry salient ?

A question that arises immediately is whether or not most firms actually possess potentially valuable asymmetries. Although this is an empirical issue, there are a number of reasons to believe that the answer is affirmative and that at the very least asymmetries are far more common and accessible than resources. First, the scope for organizational variety is vast: organizations are so complex and represent such intricate bundles of properties, people, and relationships that they are apt to be unique in countless ways (Walker, Madsen, and Carini. 2002). Indeed there are many sources of asymmetry. Long-term contracts and distinctive forms of knowledge may be consciously created. But other asymmetries in organizational systems, skill sets, processes, and even cultures evolve out of accidents of history, and unpredictable forces of intra-firm variation, selection, and retention.

Often, those differences are inimitable within the time and budget constraints demanded by a disruptive innovation challenge.

Case Study -1

Leveraging asymmetries: The Case of Shana Corp.

Shana Corp., USA, was a small, new software company. Some of its product development efforts, combined with a few technologically related contracts, had allowed the firm, over several years, to develop a budding expertise. At first, Shana's skills were not much different from most of its rivals'. But because of the kinds of jobs it had worked on (jobs richer rivals had refused), and the people it had hired to work together, Shana was acquiring an ability to develop advanced forms-completion software that could run on different computer operating systems.

Their asymmetric bundle of human and tacit knowledge resources was becoming a nascent capability. Shana's top managers gradually came to realize that their firm had learned to skillfully and cheaply do jobs that rivals could not do as well or as efficiently; nor would rivals be able to learn Shana's skills fast enough to be a threat.

Soon, Shana's managers began to develop routines, procedures, and incentive policies to further improve team performance. They also started using Shana's growing body of specialized knowledge to concentrate on clients that required its special abilities. These were typically clients that used the two popular operating systems but wanted the same forms software. This evolving market focus and the product development and marketing experience it brought sharpened Shana's expertise, widening the gap between it and its rivals. The convergence around certain skills and a target market also focused selection and training programs, project management protocols, and marketing campaigns. And it enabled Shana to exploit and extend its competitive advantage.

How to Find an Asymmetry

There are multiple avenues for discovering asymmetries—from experimentation, to self-examination and reflection. Indeed, the best firms are so managed that asymmetries are discovered and tested for potential value on an ongoing basis. Here are a few of the routes some companies have followed to find worthwhile asymmetries, the first three being less commonly described than the last.

Discovery road 1. Market contacts, experimentation and incremental learning.

Given that inimitable talent, knowledge, social systems, and client contacts exist in most organizations, it becomes a matter of experimenting to discover which of these have value, in what combinations, and where. Experimentation may take the form of exploring alternative processes, partnerships, technologies, and products. To the extent that these are indeed unique and subtle, they represent good starting places for firms to add value, find market acceptance, and earn a return. Experimentation may also involve trying different things with different clients.

Discovery Road 2. Resources, introspection, and insight.

Occasionally firms detect crucial asymmetries just by reconceptualizing their nonproductive assets. They come to view a facility or system as a potential resource not because of new way of thinking a new insight. There is a reframing of the way they perceive the organization and its components.

CASE STUDY -2

Case of Citicorp : Resources and Insight

This was the case of John Reed at Citicorp in the early 1990s. For several decades, Citi had been struggling with a global banking unit that was not only unpopular and losing ground to rivals such as Hong Kong Shanghai Bank Corp. (HSBC), but also alienating major domestic clients with poor international service. The Global Corporate Banking unit was in every respect a liability, and Reed and other managers had good reason to get rid of what was turning out to be a drain not only on reputation but also

▶

on human and financial resources. Reed, however, was not willing to give up. First, he was convinced that Citi's extensive network with banks in over 100 countries was entirely unique — no rival could match it. The closest rival, HSBC, served fewer than 40 countries. It had taken Citi decades to establish its international banking network due to legal and political obstacles, and it would take potential rivals a long time as well. Reed knew he had an inimitable asymmetry that he just might be able to turn into a resource. Second, Reed saw the trend to globalization as a long-term one, and a potential market for the network. Third, Reed believed that Citi had auxiliary talents — knowledge, contacts, and resources - that could be redirected to serve the Global Bank. Ultimately, Reed was right-he had detected an asymmetry with real potential. But as we will see, this required a great deal of 'organizational embedding' to become a capability.

Discovery road 3. Weakness, scarcity and problematic search.

Some asymmetries arise within and because of a context of weakness, and are detected or even created because of their tie to disadvantages or problems.

Disadvantages such as organizational newness, small size, inadequate capital, and a paucity of established clients can, paradoxically, drive firms into promising underserved markets and technologies of the future. The result is that firms leapfrog stronger, more established rivals (Christensen, 1997).

Case Study -3

Bypassing weakness and scarcity: Dell Computer

The young **Dell Computer** with its limited capital was compelled to begin selling computers over the phone and Internet. They did not have the finance or customer contacts, nor the political obstacles, of Compaq, IBM, or HP and were forced (and free) to embrace a different business ▶

model. The same was true for Amazon.com, which had modest resources and thus had to offer their services with only minimal bricks-and-mortar infrastructure. The result was a creative discount Internet service. Powerhouse Barnes & Noble were much slower off the mark to enter this promising market—they did not want to cannibalize their retail outlet business or alienate their agents. The same dynamic is being played out in the telecommunications industry with wireless Internet. Smaller telecoms are more willing to embrace new technology as they have fewer options and fewer constraints than, say, Deutsche Telecom with its major installed base and infrastructure. Here, the initial asymmetry, in a sense, is a willingness (indeed necessity) to pursue paths less traveled; to enter into unoccupied niches, try new approaches, and perhaps gain a foothold that leads to first-mover advantage. Asymmetries (and inimitability) here are only cognitive and political-but potentially productive, nonetheless.

Discovery road 4. Building on nascent capabilities.

In all cases, the search for asymmetries is informed by thorough and persistent inquiry across the breadth of an organization and its markets. It encompasses an evaluation of how the firm appears to differ from its competitors in the assets it possesses or in what it does well. It assesses the underlying mindsets, people, knowledge, relationships, and assets that may give rise to potential advantages. And it evaluates how asymmetries might be connected to other organizational assets, infrastructure, and market opportunities to create value (more about these last two requirements in the major sections to follow).

Challenges in Identifying Asymmetries

Asymmetries that bring advantage may be hard to detect for a number of reasons. First, they may be far removed from their favorable consequences. At Willamette Paper, for example, an apparent ability to follow the market by quickly changing grades of paper was plant flexibility, which was in turn founded in superior engineering abilities and paper plant operation, which were supported by a broad set of training and other human resources practices. It was the depth and the systemic nature of the capabilities that made them especially hard for rivals to copy — but also hard to achieve for the firm itself.

Many asymmetries also go unnoticed because they are buried within a system and are therefore subtle and causally ambiguous — even to managers of the firms that possess them. Managers know their firms are superior at some activity, but do not know why. This ignorance sometimes manifests itself in the tremendous differences in plant productivity that arise within the same organizations, which managers cannot explain. The subtlety may stem from the systemic and uncertain capabilities that underlie productivity — many drivers need to be in place, and these have to be configured just right to work together effectively.

In fact, promising asymmetries may go unrecognized because they do not generate positive outcomes. One or two subtle weaknesses — a problem of accountability, training, or morale, for instance — may hobble a state-of-the-art operational or innovative capability. For example, although Citi's branch system did represent a potentially powerful asymmetry, in 1995 it was by no means a realized capability because of key weaknesses in the organization. Other so-called capabilities are not asymmetric; they are not inimitable and thus do not confer lasting advantage. Citibank delivered excellent foreign exchange and cash management products, but so did major rivals. Shana was reliable in delivering software, but was by no means unique in that respect.

Developed capabilities may be dead ends, especially if they are tied to a single product-market opportunity, or are becoming subject to imitation by serious rivals. Nascent capabilities may be unproductive, but if developed or harnessed may hold tremendous potential for competitive advantage because they will be so unfamiliar to rivals.

Developing and supporting asymmetries

Asymmetries convert more readily into valuable resources and capabilities when embedded within a cohesive configuration. One might distinguish two kinds of configurations. The first one is composed simply of a combination of complementary asymmetries, resources and capabilities. One might contrast simple or elemental resources such as patents or a proprietary property, with a team configuration comprising a complex mix of social and technical capabilities. Such configurations may be more inimitable and robust than simple resources

The second type of configurations, however, can be especially effective when they incorporate levers of organizational design. These configurations embed asymmetries within an infrastructure that leverages, sustains, and develops them.

Organizational Design Turns Asymmetries into Capabilities

By identifying key asymmetries, managers are able to make them a high priority, fund them, and turn them into valuable resources or capabilities. Organization design can play a key role. In fact, the design of the organization may itself be one of its most profound and empowering capabilities. Design, broadly defined, is the way an organization organizes, controls, and motivates its resources to perform the most critical tasks. Its formal aspects include policies and priorities, structure (authority, task, and role definitions, accountability, liaison devices) and information, human resources, and planning systems. Informal aspects include corporate culture (values, beliefs, styles of interaction), personal contacts, and communication networks.

Structural mechanisms such as project teams, cross-functional committees, and communities of practice develop capabilities and share knowledge across different parts of the organization. They also integrate and adapt capabilities to special challenges and opportunities. Routines institutionalize knowledge and add to the stability and range of an asymmetry. Information systems target attention and monitor progress in developing an asymmetry.

Informal aspects of design are every bit as important. The *culture and values* of an organization focus effort on harnessing asymmetries and enhancing capabilities. Values define which functions or activities should receive the most support. They energize people to do better the things that matter most. And they serve as natural selection devices to attract people who best fit the company and capabilities.

Culture also gets people together informally and spontaneously to collaborate on new opportunities or unanticipated problems. It creates the *climate for interaction,* social networks, and collaboration needed to identify asymmetries and develop them into sources of advantage. Culture also can destroy organizational rites. For example. Reed's work to shift Citi's culture created a more collaborative climate that not only maximized the value of the banking system resource, but also made it less imitable. In these ways and others, organization design - often itself a sustainable advantage - becomes a central tool for unlocking, developing, and leveraging asymmetries.

Enlightened Circles Enhance Capabilities

Design elicits not only static capabilities, it launches enlightened circles that turned asymmetries into ever-growing capabilities. In a typical circle an initial asymmetry or capability attracts clients as well as very talented managers, employees, and partners — all of whom augments the capability. Capabilities also generate superior performance that in turn fuel those capabilities with more resources and attention. They also build reputation that brings opportunities, and extracts feedback from the market that helps select the right people, skills, and products. Design generally plays a key role in these virtuous circles: in identifying and prioritizing a capability, assembling the resources, people, systems and mechanisms to develop it, disseminating the capability within the organization, and in leveraging it across the right market opportunities.

CASE STUDY - 4

Capability Enhancing Assymetry : ISS

Denmark 's International Service System (ISS) is one of the largest service firms in the world. In its early years the company accepted contracts for cleaning abattoirs. This was a challenging job as complex equipment had to be dismantled for cleaning, and special disinfectants and pressurized cleaning techniques were needed to exterminate different varieties of bacteria. Also vital was expertise in sterility testing. Experience with different types of clients eventually enabled ISS to develop unusually efficient routines for doing the work, as well as the ability to cost and price cleaning services by machine, square meter, or type of food. Moreover, their proprietary technical knowledge in food hygiene enabled ISS to form partnerships with clients to develop procedures for evolving types of bacteria. This enhanced skills, giving ISS even greater advantage and expanding the client base. Ultimately, expertise grew to encompass related hygiene-food businesses such as poultry and fish (Galbraith, 2000a). Organization design fueled the circle. Leaders, for example, realizing the benefits of focus, tried to acquire 'customer density' in special market segments. Scale in a segment led both to buying power and greater specialization, with resulting learning and customer intimacy advantages. Leaders also prioritized opportunities that were coining within range because of growing skills or reputation. Databases were then evolved on costs and customers that facilitated better pricing and scheduling, while human resource systems codified selection and training criteria.

Technical capabilities could draw the most talented employees as word gets out about a company's prowess. Winners get to choose the best teams—and their experience guide them what kinds of teams to pick. Also, as capabilities become apparent to desirable business partners, joint development efforts are launched that grow those capabilities. This is known as capability cycle.

Another virtuous cycle starts with reputation resources. A reputation for style or quality could draw prestigious clients whose patronage enhance reputation still further. Or a reputation for technical excellence could attract talented alliance partners, scientists, or engineers, who then boost reputation-and of course capabilities—still further. So capability and reputation cycles reinforce one another. Table - 4 gives the strategy to use asymmetry

Table 4 : Strategy for use of asymmetry

1.	Discover the asymmetries-however minor however buried, however troubled - and discern the potential within them.
2.	Turn asymmetries into capabilities by strategically embedding them within an organizational design configuration that exploits them and sustains their development.
3.	Match asymmetry-derived capabilities to market opportunities.

New Growth May Not Be Visible but Present

One of the reasons it is so difficult for managers in established companies to recognize disruptions as opportunities is that the new markets lie outside their existing resource base. They may see a market developing but incorrectly conclude that it is outside their company's scope for products or customers. In the early days of the minicomputer, for example, IBM Corp. hired a leading consulting firm to gauge the size of the emerging market. The firm's report concluded that no opportunity existed for IBM - a predictable outcome, given that the firm had surveyed IBM's leading customers, who were happy with performance enough to be able to meet the demands of most customers in the mainframe market at a significantly lower cost. Mainframe manufacturers responded by continuing to move upmarket toward more complex, higher-margin products. In phase three, they had nowhere left to go, and the

mainframe market began to decline. Mainframe companies began to provide more than the mainstream market could absorb; their cost structures made it impossible for them to compete effectively with minicomputer makers for that market. At the beginning of this phase, the total market for minicomputers permanently surpassed that of mainframes. (See "Minicomputers Disrupt Mainframes.") Surprisingly, perhaps, there is good news in this scenario for incumbents. Although revenues from the minicomputer market first surpassed the mainframe computer market in 1984, they did not sustain that lead until the early 1990s — almost 35 years after the launch of the minicomputer market. The mainframe market grew rapidly for nearly 20 years and then more slowly for about even more; even now, the mainframe market still generates more than $6 billion in revenue annually. But it has entered a long period of decline Although a disruption may not completely destroy the established business, it usually takes away all the growth.
The figure-3. shows a schematic of disruptor-incumbent market situation.

New Customers – Where Are They?

The first step in locating new customers is identifying a new market. Managers can use three criteria to do that: First, the disruptive innovation must be undervalued by current customers. Second, it must compete against nonconsumption; that is, it must allow people to do things they couldn't do in the past for lack of money or skill. And third, it must help people accomplish things that they are already trying to do but can't with the available products or services.

By using these criteria, executives can develop the intuition they need to look outside their established markets for customers in a disruptive market. An example from the health care industry demonstrates how this can work.

Consider how treatment of heart disease has evolved. Before the 1960s, a person whose lifetime love of greasy food left him with

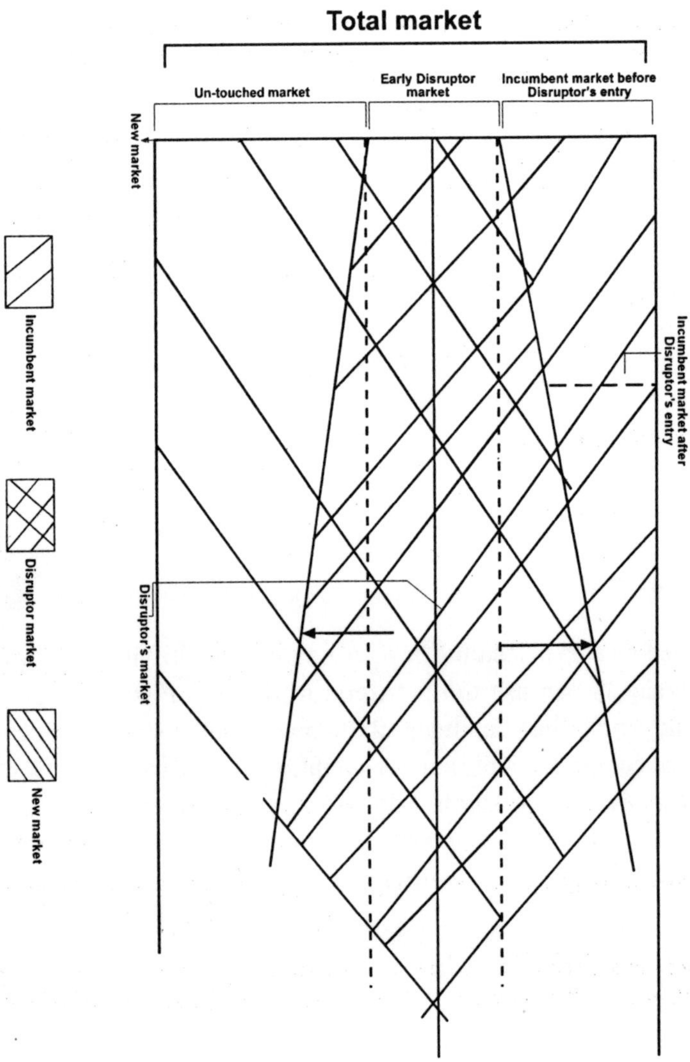

Fig. 3 Incumbent-Disruptor Market Situation.

coronary artery disease and extreme chest pain could do little more than take crude medications and hope for the best. Then coronary bypass surgery, which rerouted blood flow around a blocked heart vessel, literally gave the gift of life to thousands. That gift, however, came at a price. The operation, performed by a highly trained cardiac surgeon, was very invasive. It consisted of "cracking" the chest — literally sawing and separating the rib cage so the surgeon could have direct access to the heart. To permit the delicate sewing of the bypass graft (usually a vein from the leg), the heart had to be stopped completely. A complicated system of tubing, reservoirs, filters and other devices called a perfusion circuit played the role of the heart and lungs during the operation. Recovery time from the operation was fairly lengthy, and the pain was sometimes intense, often at the place in the leg where the vein had been harvested. For those patients with severe and sometimes multiple blockages, however, the procedure was a godsend.

Few cardiac surgeons paid much attention when Andreas Gruentzig, a young German physician, performed the first balloon angioplasty procedure in 1974. In this procedure, the doctor guided a catheter through an artery into the blocked coronary artery and then briefly inflated a tiny balloon; the balloon compressed the plaque that was keeping the artery partially or completely closed and was then withdrawn with the catheter. This procedure was far less invasive and the recovery was far less painful than bypass surgery. Cardiac surgeons were understandably not interested when balloon angioplasty was introduced — it was a highly inferior solution for their core group of patients (whose heart disease was too far advanced to be treated in that way) and was reimbursed at a lower rate. But the procedure was embraced by another group, cardiologists, who valued the approach for its potential to expand their very different scope of practice. In addition, they were reimbursed for performing balloon angioplasties at a rate higher than they received for such customary procedures as angiograms. Thus balloon angioplasty created an entirely new market for patients unable to tolerate complex and invasive surgery and for those with less serious blockages. (See "Disruption in Cardiovascular Surgery.")

Through the early 1990s, both balloon angioplasty and bypass procedures grew in tandem — phase one of the disruption. But angioplasty then became a much-improved option for patient care. One of its principal drawbacks until that time was its high level of restenosis, a renarrowing of the artery after the procedure. The introduction of stents — small cylindrical cages that remain in the vessel and keep it propped open — greatly reduced this problem.

CASE STUDY - 5

Minicomputers Disrupt Mainframes

Minicomputers eventually displaced a significant chunk of the mainframe business — but it took nearly 40 years before the disruptive technology established a sustained lead in revenues. Mainframe manufacturers moved their products upmarket in phases one and two until they had no place left to go in phase three.

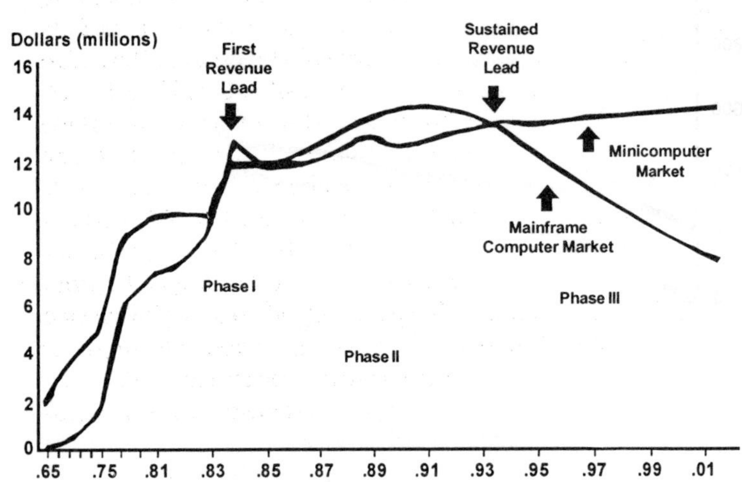

Fig. 4 Growth of mini computer market
SOURCE : Information Technology Industry Council, USA

Case Study - 6

Disruption in Cardiovascular Surgery

As with other forms of disruption, new customers have led the way in which heart treatment has changed over the past 20 years. The patients who could not withstand or did not need bypass surgery were the initial customers for the balloon angioplasty procedure. Cardiologists were the caregivers who performed the procedure itself, not the cardiac surgeons who were performing bypass surgery in the established market. Phase one of this disruption ended in 1995. when the advent of stenting began phase two. technical advances, demand for angioplasty began to soar, increasingly to the benefit of patients who in the past would have been candidates for bypass surgery — phase two of the disruption.

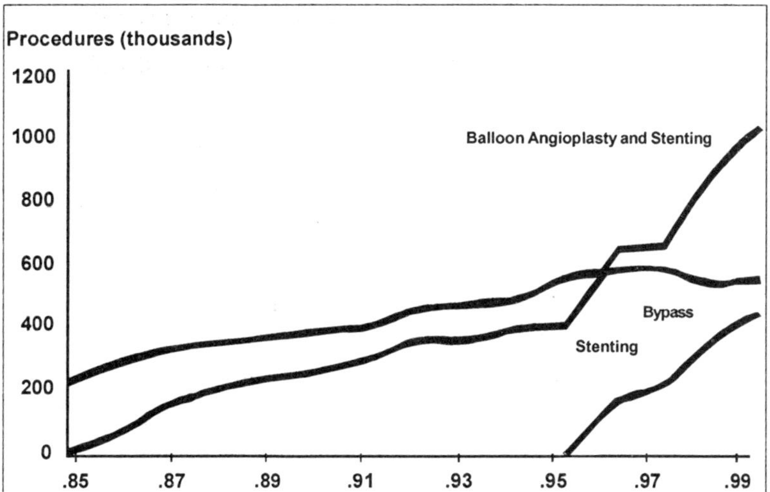

Fig. 5 Growth of balloon angioplasty market
SOURCE: American Heart Association

As in other instances of disruption, those who dominate the new market for heart treatments are not those who led the old one. Cardiac surgeons today are very good at treating patients with the most critical needs, but they've missed the opportunity to capitalize on balloon angioplasty. Cardiologists have seized this market and found a large group of new customers who can be treated with the new technology.

New Business Models Cater to New Customers

Customers in a disruptive market can't be served according to the established market's business model. Cardiologists were able to serve new patients profitably and routinely with balloon angioplasty, thanks to an ability to do many more procedures per year with less staff in comparison to bypass surgery. Similarly, minicomputer companies could profitably serve their customers at gross margins lower than those of mainframe manufacturers because their selling costs were lower, their inventory turned quicker, and their fixed costs were a lower percentage of their total business.

But established players, which often have trouble seeing the new customer in the first place, also often find it difficult to conceptualize the new business model that would allow them to serve a new market profitably. The print newspaper industry illustrates how a focus on established customers can blind companies to business-model changes being led by new customers in a disruptive market.

As digital publishing took off in the mid-1990s, many newspaper companies spent millions of dollars designing and marketing their Web sites. Their stated motivation was almost exclusively to protect the newspapers' print franchise. They were concerned that both readers and advertisers would move online, leaving them with lower revenues to cover their high fixed production and distribution costs. Most online newspapers simply replicated their print business model, trying to sell blocks of online advertising space to their usual customers: department stores, car dealers and other retailers that were not interested in exploring the benefits of interactive media at that time. In doing so, the newspapers initially missed the opportunity to reach advertisers that were trying to target individuals with customized messages. Most new entrants into online media such as Yahoo!, Monster.com and CNET built business models that captured the interactive opportunity. But more importantly, they sold ad space to advertisers that had not traditionally advertised in the established newspaper market, especially companies that run direct-to-consumer campaigns. Newspapers, despite the functionality provided by IBM's mainframes. Five years later, minicomputers were a billion-dollar business.

Similarly, the CEO of a leading disk-drive manufacturer was once asked about the potential of an emerging product to disrupt his company's established position. He responded, "I've read the reports, but I tell you the numbers are not there. We've surveyed our customers and nobody is buying those things. I'm telling you, someone is making those numbers up!" But the numbers were real, and the emerging market soon became a multimillion-dollar opportunity that this incumbent missed out on. At the root of these examples is the reality that the growth associated with disruption originates in a space in the market not traditionally served by the established players. The new customers are initially different, as is the way they use the product, making it difficult for established companies to recognize the opportunity with their existing systems.

Incumbents fail to see how they might take advantage of the new market and often mistakenly assume that the disruption will immediately displace their established business. Eastman Kodak Co., for example, has spent billions responding to digital photography. Fearing that digital newcomers would attack directly, Kodak's first commercial effort in this market was to install more than 2,000 digital printing kiosks in its established retail distribution channel of pharmacies and grocery chains. Kodak was thus competing head-on with its own chemical film business. But the initial customer adoption of digital photography came through home and game applications — new customers seeking new applications. Digital photography will eventually attack the chemical film market, but it is growing initially in an area entirely outside the established market.

Disruption As an Opportunity for Growth

Although a disruptive business will eventually attack established markets (the area of displacement), it originates in a space outside the existing markets. This creates a large area of new net growth, even as the new business expands (see figure.6).

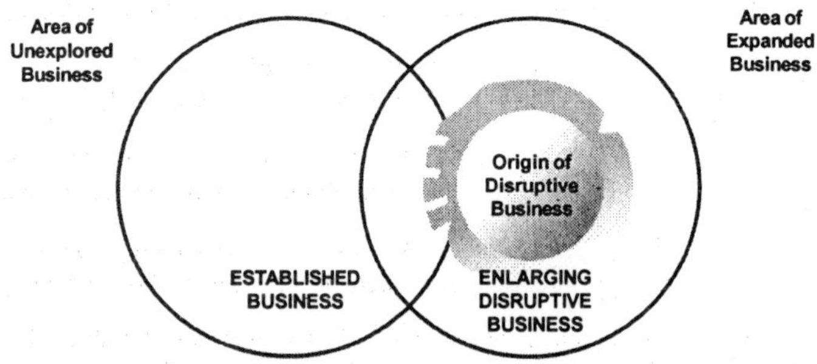

Fig. 6 Disruptive business may originate outside the established business

Case Study - 7

HLL-Nirma contest

(Hindustan Lever Ltd. (HLL), a subsidiary of Great Britain's Unilever PLC and widely considered the best-managed company in India, has been a pioneer among MNCs exploring markets. For more than 50 years, HLL has served India's small elite who could afford to buy MNC products. In the 1990s, a local firm, Nirma Ltd., began offering detergent products

▶

for poor consumers, mostly in rural areas. In fact, Nirma created a new business system that included a new product formulation, low-cost manufacturing process, wide distribution network, special packaging for daily purchasing, and value pricing.

HLL, in typical MNC fashion, initially dismissed Nirma's strategy. However, as Nirma grew rapidly, HLL could see its local competitor was winning in a market it had disregarded. Ultimately, HLL saw its vulnerability and its opportunity: In 1995, the company responded with its own offering for this market, drastically altering its traditional business model.

HLL's new detergent, called Wheel, was formulated to substantially reduce the ratio of oil to water in the product, responding to the fact that the poor often wash their clothes in rivers and other public water systems. HLL decentralized the production, marketing, and distribution of the product to leverage the abundant labor pool in rural India, quickly creating sales channels through the thousands of small outlets where low-income people shop. HLL also changed the cost structure of its detergent business so it could introduce Wheel at a low price point.

Today, Nirma and HLL are close competitors in the detergent market, with 38 percent market share each, according to IndiaInfoline.com, a business intelligence and market research service. New market is not a market that allows for the traditional pursuit of high margins; instead, profits are driven by volume and capital efficiency. Margins are likely to be low (by current norms), but unit sales can be extremely high. Managers who focus on gross margins will miss the opportunity at the bottom of the pyramid; managers who innovate and focus on economic profit will be rewarded.

Nirma has become one of the largest branded detergent makers in the world. Meanwhile, HLL, stimulated by its emergent rival and its changed business model, registered a 20 percent growth in revenues per year and a 25 percent growth in profits per year between 1995 and 2000. Over the same period, HLL's market capitalization grew to $12 billion — a growth

▶

rate of 40 percent per year. HLL's parent company, Unilever, also has benefited from its subsidiary's experience in India. Unilever transported HLL's business principles (not the product or the brand) to create a new detergent market among the poor in Brazil, where the Ala brand has been a big success. More important, Unilever has adopted the bottom of the pyramid as a corporate strategic priority. As the Unilever example makes clear, the starting assumption must be that serving low income people involves bringing together the best of technology and a global resource base to address local market conditions. Cheap and low-quality products are not the goal. The potential of bottom segment of the market cannot be realized without an entrepreneurial orientation: The real strategic challenge for managers is to visualize an active market where only abject poverty exists today. It takes tremendous imagination and creativity to engineer a market infrastructure out of a completely unorganized sector.

Case Study - 8

Disruptive Strategy to add growth in the market: ITC's e-chaupal

ITC's game plan by e-chaupal is a unique venture of creating new market by distruptive strategy. In 1999, ITC could recognise that much of the sonsumer growth in the Indian cities can be replicated in village India if in addition to marketing its product it also helps the farming community in getting some added capital to buy its products. So more the farmers get benefited by means of increased capital, better price of their products, better seeds and professional help; more they will be in a position to buy ITC or its franchisee products. ITC runs computer kiosks, known locally as e-chaupals in the Indian rural hinterland where ITC helps the farmer to know the price of commodities, fertilizers, pesticides and seeds etc. By this empowerment ITC value addition proposition will keep adding up and it plans to sell other products and services through this route. It is a perfect case of disruption because till this time, ITC's competitors only thought of rural marketing as the only method of increased sales. Its incumbent competitor, HLL, the Indian associate of Unilever PLC within

▶

this time could only think of a penetrative rural marketing program, "Shakti" whereby it selected a woman or a self-help group, quite in the same way Amway began door-todoor-sales, in a cluster of villages to sell its products but volume of business remains a problem. In contrast, ITC's e-chaupal not only grew in size but also has been a darling of the Indian government (as seen from the score of prizes it deservedly won) as well benefited from no or little tax of transactions in the rural area.

ITC's e-chaupal business is estimated to grow from Rs. 850 crores ($ 175 million) today to Rs. 7000 crores ($ 1.5 billion) in 2010 almost at a phenomenal growth rate of 160% every year. In contrast project "Shakti" is expected to grow in the same segment from Rs. 100 crores ($ 22 million) to Rs. 1000 crores ($ 220 million) e-chaupal will cover from 5050 kiosks in 31000 villages today to 20,000 kiosks in 1,00,000 Indian villages, by 2010.

Table 5 : New Strategies for the bottom segment of the market

Price Performance	Views of Quality
• Product development • Manufacturing • Distribution	• New delivery formats • Creation of robust products for harsh conditions (heat, dust, etc.)
Sustainability	**Profitability**
• Reduction in resource intensity • Recyclability • Renewable energy	• Investment intensity • Margins • Volume

Road Mapping Disruptive Threats

Roadmaps and roadmapping can be divided into two activities. First, the selection of a type of roadmap to properly display trends and interactions is required. Options for the type of roadmap are many, including market, product, and core technology roadmaps. Second, a means for the identification of entries for incorporation in the roadmap is required. The tools of technology forecasting are employed to establish what technology trends will actually occur and when they will occur.

This division is shown schematically in Fig. 7. Based on this division, it is interesting to note that, in many respects, technology roadmapping is similar to geographic mapping, where decisions regarding the nature of the map (ranging from political to topographic to weather) and the imaging technique employed to generate entries in the map (ranging from census taking to traditional surveying to satellite imaging) are required. The figures 8 & 9 explain the phases of technology and disruptive technology roadmapping processes.

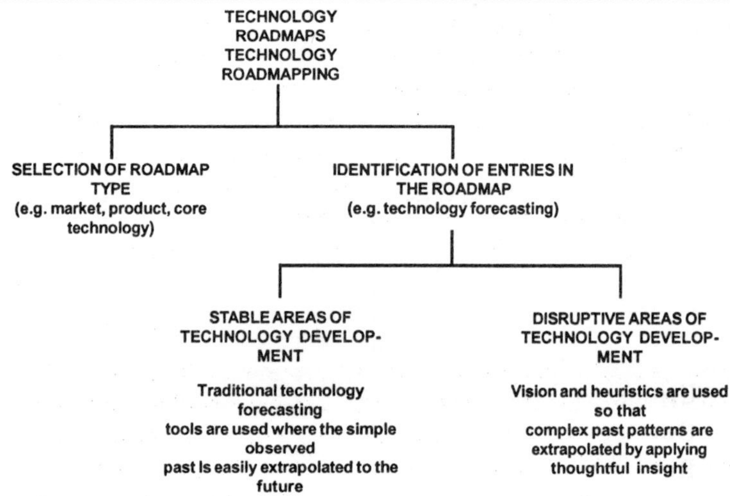

Fig. 7 Hierarchy of technology roadmapping. The SAILS methodology fits within the activity of identification of disruptive entries into the roadmap. (Vojak et al, 2004) SAILS - Standards, Architechture, Integration, Linkages and Substitution

Phase I: Preliminary Activity

↓

1. Satisfy essential conditions.
2. Provide leadership/sponsorship.
3. Define the scope and boundaries.

Phase II: Development of the Technology Roadmap

↓

1. Identify the "product" that will be the focus of the roadmap
2. Identify the critical system requirements and their targets.
3. Specify the technology drivers and their targets.
5. Identify technology alternatives and their time lines.
6. Recommend the technology alternatives that should be pursued.
7. Create the technology roadmap report.

Phase III: Follow-up Activity

↓

1. Critique and validate the technology roadmap.
2. Develop an implementation plan.
3. Review and update

Fig. 8 The three phases in the technology roadmapping process (Walsh, 2004).

Phase I: Preliminary Activity

↓

1. Satisfy essential conditions.
2. Provide leadership/sponsorship from multiple segments of value chain.
3. Define the scope and boundaries.
4. *Understand the nature of disruptive technologies.*

Phase II: Development of the Technology Roadmap

↓

1. *Identify promising "Technology-Product" paradigms.*
2. *Develop " Holy Grail" Grand Challenges.*
3. *Identify and categorize major technology pathways.*
4. *Specify relative technologies infrastructure positions.*
5. *Specify nomenclature and glossary activities, mini-roadmap standards.*
6. *Identify specific technology segments for "mini-roadmaps".*
7. *Create ability for others to utilize output for their own roadmaps.*
8. *Create the technology roadmap report.*

Phase III: Follow-up Activity

↓

1. Critique and validate the technology roadmap.
2. Develop an implementation plan.
3. Review and update.
4. *Seek transition timing to Sustaining Roadmap.*

Fig. 9 Disruptive technology industry roadmapping process (Walsh, 2004).

Note : Observe disruption technology roadmapping is different from evolutionary technology roadmapping as in figure - 8).

SAILS

Working on technology roadmapping Vojak et al (2004) identified the heirarchy in the disruptive technology roadmapping process, as in figure - 9.

A methodology offered by Vojak et al (2004) identifies five different types of disruptive contributors commonly observed at the subsystem level, those due to :

- Changes in Industry Standards.
- Changes in Architectures,
- Various forms of Integration and Disintegration of elements,
- Linkages between various elements across the supersystem, and
- Substitutions within the subsystem.

Industry standards set a specification for the performance of an element or an element of a supersystem at some level in the hierarchy. As such, standards provide a set of performance definitions without necessarily specifying how the performance is to be obtained. Additionally, the internal changes brought about by changes in standards often lead to further opportunity for disruptive changes at the subsystem level.

Widely adopted standards provide a consistent framework within which to innovate and potentially disrupt. This is especially true in standards-driven industry segments, e.g., data communications and telecommunications, or the automotive industry, where commercial success requires adherence to standards, often to ensure interoperability among equipment offered by different vendors. The standards for the output of modems, for example, allowed the substitution of integrated sound/modem ICs, such as Rockwell's, or even the use of the processor itself in PCs, Winmodems, for the generation of the correct signals. This was disruptive to the dedicated modem products and provided significant cost savings to the end user. Close monitoring of standards activities can provide an early warning of a potential disruption.

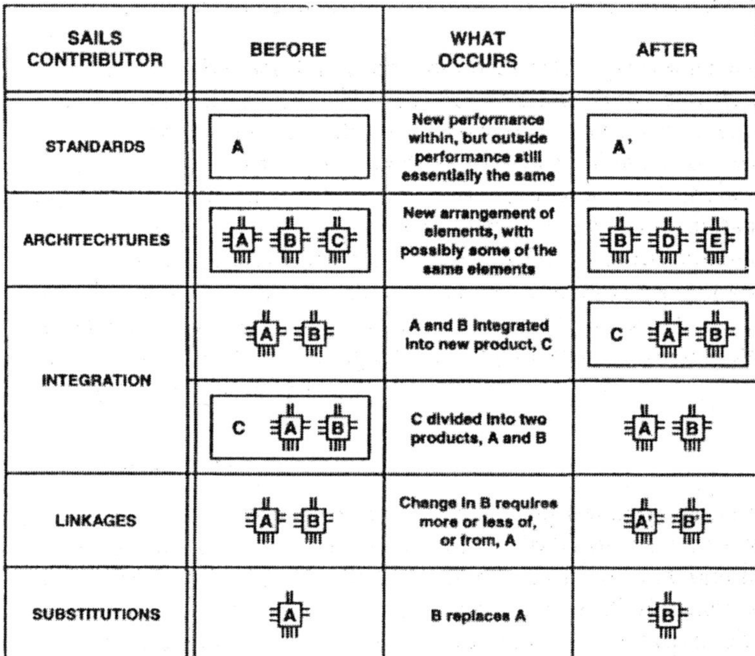

Fig. 10 Summary of the five components of the SAILS methodology (Vojak et al, 2004).

Architectural changes occur when a subsystem, system or supersystem performs the same function with different elemental technology. Inputs, outputs, and key functionality are essentially maintained, but a new arrangement or combination of the internal elements is used to accomplish this end goal. This area can be strongly influenced by the existence of standards at some level in the systems hierarchy. Per Fig. 10, a new arrangement of elements, with possibly some of the same elements as before, is used to accomplish the same end goal.

Integration broadly covers a wide range of activity, including:

- integration - combining several constituent elements to form a new subsystem,
- disintegration - separating a subsystem into its constituent elements, and

- reintegration - combining a new subset of constituent elements after disintegration

To accomplish integration, the designer must look for commonality of technology and function in all elements, for example, the integration of multimedia and modem functionality mentioned earlier. Note that this threat or opportunity can be used against suppliers (backward integration), customers (forward integration), and makers of other elements in a subsystem (lateral integration). Further, it is important to note that this threat or opportunity can come from more than one level of the value chain away from the element under consideration. Integration can also be used to take advantage of process technologies, e.g., the integration of the serializer/deserializer function with the drivers for optical communications on the same chip.

In his seminal work on competitive advantage, Porter (1985) discusses the concept of linkages both within the value chain and with other levels of the value chain. Linkages are defined as "relationships between the way one value activity is performed and the cost or performance of another" Porter illustrates this concept with the example of moving from metal to sintered, net shape ceramic engine parts. The process of doing so eliminates the need for machining of parts and, as such, serves to compete with suppliers of machined metal parts. Linkages can result from increases of the functionality of an element in one part of a supersystem causing either increases or decreases of the functionality or requirement for other elements in the supersystem. Similarly, decreases in the functionality of an element in one part of a supersystem can cause either increases or decreases of the functionality or requirement for other elements.

Porter has identified linkages within the value chain and with other levels of the value chain as crucial, but often subtle and unrecognized. Further, he goes on to point out that "managing linkages is a more complex organizational task than managing value activities themselves" and that "given the difficulty of recognizing and managing linkages, the ability to do so often yields a sustainable source of competitive advantage" This concept of linkages can be adapted from its application in business systems to complex, technology-based subsystems. The identification of linkages in complex, technology-based subsystems is as challenging a task as Porter suggests it is in a business system and offers similar potential disruptive competitive advantage. For example, the increasing intelligence of test instrumentation has enabled increased functionality in the area of data handling. By providing database-like functions in the instrument itself, entire layers in the customer's information storage and handling chain can be eliminated with little additional development cost and essentially no added manufacturing cost. This can be very disruptive to suppliers at the next level in the chain.

Finally, substitutions occur when a radical technology replacement is made in the same or similar environment. This can be, for example, a material or component performing the same function with different technology. For example, the substitution of optical data links for electrical wires or cables in communications systems is a simple example of the concept of substitution.

In one area, where the disruption is much prevalent is the mobile telephoney sector where micro electro-mechanical systems (MEMS) powered by tiny moving parts inside them, rule. An infrastructure building model for disruptive opportunity by both technology push and market pull can be seen as figure - 11.

The challenge of implementing any methodology such as this is to cast the net broadly enough to identify as many realistic competitive opportunities as possible while not being ridiculous in the scope of analysis. One way to implement this is to first identify the bill of materials for the subsystem under consideration (i.e., the company's product) as well as for the entire supersystem that it operates within. Then each of the methodology steps can, in turn, be considered not only for the subsystem but also for the various elements of the subsystem.

The job of the design engineer, then, is to systematically analyze the subsystem and supersystem bills of materials applying the following five perspectives (Vojak et al, 2004).

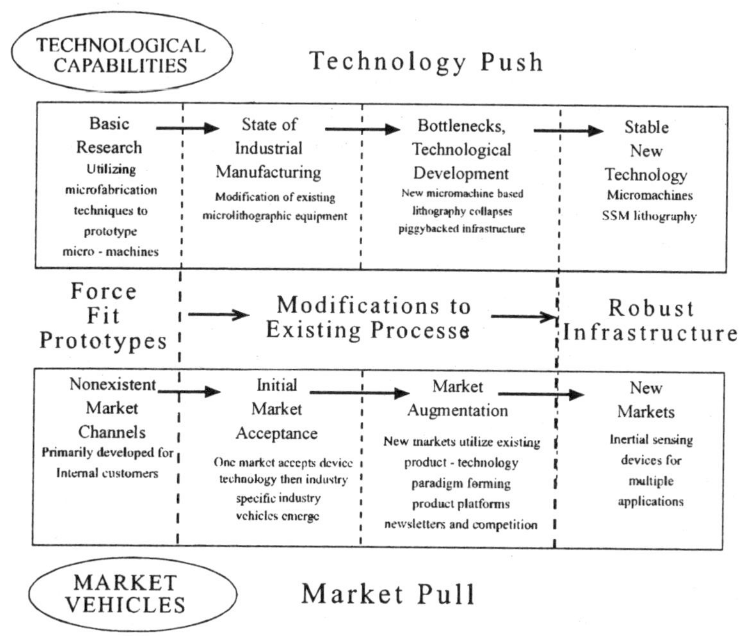

Fig. 11 An Example of Infrastructure for disruptive technologies. Micro-electro-mechanical machine systems (MEMS).

Standards

The process begins with the designer seeking to understand what the trends are for industry standardization at various levels of the value-added chain and how they impact product performance characteristics. Participation in the standards process is an excellent way to accomplish this. Off-line conversations and proposals can provide significant insight.

Architecture

The designer next moves to brainstorming various architecture options available at each value-added level within the supersystem. These first two steps set the stage for the rest of the analysis.

Integration

The burden on the designer here is to develop options for forward integration, backward integration, and lateral integration into the rest of the supersystem. It also involves putting oneself in the position of the designer of other portions of the supersystem and determining to what extent your product (or some portion of the function of your product) could be a target of their attack. This part of the analysis must be repeated for each standard and architecture option under consideration. In addition, various sequences and combinations of disintegration and reintegration must necessarily be considered. Often a blank paper approach to meeting the system or subsystem requirements is helpful.

Linkages

Perhaps the most difficult (and most rewarding) task is the identification of linkages between the functional performance of all portions of the product with the performance of all other elements of the supersystem. This part of the analysis also must be repeated for each standard and architecture option under consideration.

Substitutions

This step is challenging in that it requires the designer to seek out what he or she may currently not be aware of, competitive threats to a component of your product or some portion of the product that may radically replace that element. As much as with the other elements of the methodology, this requires a proactive scanning of the technical literature to know what is out there, as well as to evaluate the level of threat or opportunity it provides. The net must be cast very widely as the most disruptive substitutions can occur quickly through the adoption of a component or subsystem that has already been developed for a very different application

CASE STUDY - 9

Optical multiplexing subsystems in optical communication supersystems

A typical optical communication system multiplexes large numbers of voice and data streams into a high-speed optical channel, transmits the information, and breaks it back out into its constituent streams at the receiving end, demultiplexing. The introduction of dense wavelength division multiplexing (DWDM) is a good example of the introduction of a disruptive technology at the systems level in this industry. To understand why this technology was disruptive, we first look at an optical system prior to the introduction of DWDM (Fig. 12). In this system, information is multiplexed, concentrated, at the central office and possibly at intermediate points in the system. Each set of multiplexed signals is converted to light in a transmitter and propagated through an optical fiber to the receiving central office where it is converted back into an electrical signal, demultiplexed, and sent to the intended receiver.

The introduction of two technological advances enabled major changes in the system. The first was the fiber amplifier. Alone, it is disruptive, as it replaces repeaters and extends the distance a signal can be transmitted without reconstitution. More important, it is broadband, enabling the use of the second advance, narrow-line-width lasers. These devices use less than 1% of the optical spectrum that a standard laser uses. In early systems, additional capacity was gained by using both of the transmission windows centered around 1310 and 1550 nm in the optical fiber (Fig. 12). The introduction of both of these technologies allowed many independent optical signals to be sent over a single fiber. The fact that the amplifier is practical in only the 1550-nm window meant that the 1310-nm window would only be used for short links, if at all, as system capacities were increased. An additional impact is that with DWDM far fewer fibers are needed for the same total bandwidth.

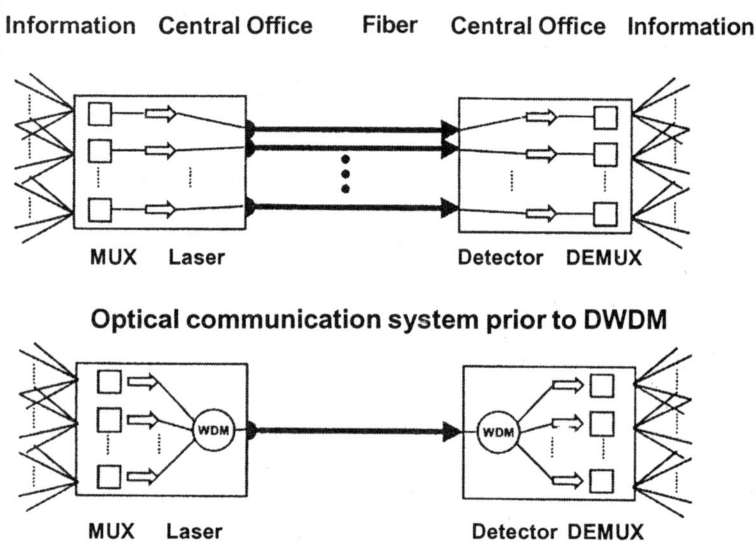

Fig. 12 Optical communication system after introduction of DWDM

Human Resources

Managers who have successfully worked their way up the ladder of a stable business unit—for example, a division that manufactures standard high-volume electric motors for the appliance industry—are likely to have acquired the skills that were necessary to succeed in that context. The "graduates" of this school would have finely honed operational skills in managing quality programs, process improvement teams, and cost-control efforts. Even the most senior manufacturing executives from such a school would likely be weak, however, in starting up a new plant, because one encounters very different problems in starting up a *new* plant than in running a well-tuned one.

When a slowly growing firm's leaders decide they need to launch a new-growth business to restore their company's vitality, who should they tap to head the venture? A talented manager from the core business who has demonstrated a record of success? An outsider who has started and grown a successful company? The school-of-experience view suggests that both of these managers might be risky hires. The internal candidate would have learned how to meet budgeted numbers, negotiate major supply contracts, and improve operational efficiency and quality, but might not have attended any "courses" on starting a new business in his or her prior career assignments. An outside entrepreneur might have learned a lot about building new fast-moving organizations, but would have little experience competing for resources and bucking inappropriate processes within a stable, efficiency-oriented operating culture.

Right Managers for Disruptive Growth

In order to be confident that managers have developed the skills required to succeed at a new assignment, one should examine the sorts of problems they have wrestled with in the past. It is not as important that managers have succeeded with the problem as it is for them to have wrestled with it and developed the skills and intuition for how to meet the challenge successfully the next time around. One problem with predicting future success from past success is that managers can succeed for reasons not of their own making—and we often learn far more from our failures than our successes. Failure and bouncing back from failure can be critical courses in the school of experience. As long as they are willing and able to learn, doing things wrong and recovering from mistakes can give managers an instinct for better navigating through the minefield the next time around.

Case Study - 10

Strategy went wrong: Intel-SAP Joint Venture

Pandesic, the high-profile joint venture between Intel and SAP that was launched in 1997 to create a new-market disruption selling enterprise resource planning (ERP) software to small businesses. Intel and SAP hand-picked some of their most successful, tried-and-true executives to lead the venture. ▶

Pandesic ramped to 100 employees in eight months, and quickly established offices in Europe and Asia. Within a year it had announced forty strategic partnerships with companies such as Compaq, Hewlett-Packard, and Citibank. The company inked distribution and implementation agreements with the same IT consulting firms that had served as such capable channel partners for SAP's large-company systems. The product, initially intended to be simple ERP software delivered to small businesses via the Internet, evolved into a completely automated end-to-end solution. Pandesic was a spectacular failure. It sold very few systems and shut its doors in February 2001 after having spent more than $100 million.

One of the most vexing dilemmas that stable corporations face when they seek to rekindle growth by launching new businesses is that their internal schools of experience have offered precious few courses in which managers could have learned how to launch new disruptive businesses. In many ways, the managers that corporate executives have come to trust the most because they have consistently delivered the needed results in the core businesses cannot be trusted to shepherd the creation of new growth. Human resources executives in this situation need to shoulder a major burden. They need to monitor where in the corporation's schools of experience the needed courses might be created, and ensure that promising managers have the opportunity to be appropriately schooled before they are asked to take the helm of a new-growth business. When managers with the requisite education cannot be found internally, they need to ensure that the management team, as a balanced composite, has within it the requisite perspectives from the right schools of experience. We will return to this challenge later in this chapter.

Finding managers who have been appropriately schooled is a critical first step in assembling the capabilities required to succeed. But it is only the first step, because the capabilities of organizations are a function of resources other than people, and of elements beyond just resources, namely, processes and values.

Managerial Lessons

There are a few of the lessons managers must take to heart if they are to capture the new growth associated with disruptive innovation.

First, disruption creates new net growth. The key is to focus on the combined net effect of growth rather than the potential losses in one market.

Second, new customers must be found outside the established market. Disruptive innovations serve those who are currently nonconsuming but want to move upmarket and accomplish things they can't with available products or services.

Third, disruptive technology is never disruptive to the customers who buy it. Balloon angioplasty was viewed as a poor solution to heart disease by cardiac surgeons but as a breakthrough by cardiologists. Part of the key to successful disruptive innovation is finding customers who will more than welcome it, even if it delivers less than the standard in the established market.

Fourth, products should be built according to the outcomes demanded by the new market, and the legacy costs and undervalued features associated with the established products should be abandoned.

Finally, a disruptive new business should start small and not be forced to grow quickly. Starting small enables managers to figure out what the new customers require and don't require, adjusting business models and product architectures early before huge resources are poured into the new business. It also eases pressures to make the disruption conform to the established market.

Case Study -11

Infosys, the successful Disruptive Innovator: Narayana Murthy-Christensen Discourse

"As long as Infosys innovates, it will survive and succeed," N R Narayana

▶

Murthy, chairman and chief mentor of Infosys once said. "The day it stops, it will disappear like dew on a sunny morning." Says Christensen: "Infosys's business model is disruptive relative to the IT services industry in North America and Europe." What made Infosys's Global Delivery Model (GDM) disruptive was its framework for distributed project management, the ability to deploy multi-location, multi-time-zone teams to execute projects efficiently and at low cost. Like all disrupters, Infosys moved up the value ladder by deploying the model better, faster, more efficiently and in more areas. The company evolved from writing small bits of code "offshore" at its Bangalore office to IT consulting to business process outsourcing. Now the company is gearing up for the next level, a new initiative called Thousand Board-Room Consultants. Moving up the ladder has not only improved Infosys's margins but it has also helped the company integrate more with its customers' needs. "It's exactly the right strategy for Infosys to follow. It does have to move up the ladder," says Christensen. "However, while the move to create Infosys was a disruptive innovation, all the improvements in Infosys's ability to execute faster, better and more complicated IT solutions are sustaining innovations. As it moves up the ladder and becomes more and more integrated, Infosys needs to create something that has a proprietary interdependent architecture inside its product offering. Only that will allow Infosys to unleash a disruptive product or service that will become its ticket to the club of global IT companies. Infosys is to foster innovation and he points to the company's Software, Engineering & Technology (SET) Lab. "Our people there read, import all kinds of technologies, and come up with ideas. The ideas are discussed with people in the field, and they try to integrate them on an incremental basis" Clearly, any idea that comes out of the SET Lab has to fit into Infosys's current scheme of things; sustaining innovations that help Infosys do what it currently does, better, faster, or cheaper. By mandate, SET Labs can never produce truly disruptive ideas — ideas for the future that threaten Infosys's current business model. : Infosys could also forego speedy growth if its quest for disruptive innovations is restricted to low-end disruptions based on leveraging lower costs. Christensen's response: "A new-market disruption would be for Infosys to say, well, the best microprocessor

▶

design capability resides in Intel. What Infosys will do is create a set of design rules that make it possible for software engineers to design microprocessors that are optimised to run software. That will make it possible for software engineers to custom configure microprocessors to optimise the applications they are running. That would be a disruptive innovation. It would enable a larger population of engineers, who historically couldn't, design microprocessors because Infosys made it rules-based and modular."

Lulled by success, Infosys could ignore its quest for new market disruption until it is too late. Says Christensen: "Right now Infosys is at the top of its game. But, in five years, you can bet that Infosys will begin to see some maturity in its core business. At that stage, it will want to find another growth business that is becoming very large. If Infosys wants to have such a business five years from now, it has to start it today. If it waits until the numbers look bad, that will be too late." What makes Infosys particularly vulnerable to disruption is its low-cost plank. Accepts Murthy: "I entirely agree with Christensen that if you play only the game of low-cost disruption, then the victor today will become the victim tomorrow." Luckily for Infosys, the solutions are within reach. If it wishes, its recent foray into RFID (radio frequency identification) could be just the big disruptive innovation it needs. The technology has potential to replace bar codes one day. Infosys could either treat RFID as yet another area to dabble in for small gains, or an opportunity to develop a revolutionary new product for smarter supply chain management.

The Turnaround of the Incumbent

Though most researchers believe that the existing entreprenuers, or incumbents will have late-mover dis-advantage, there is yet another view that runs against the disruptor-winner view. Although the standard model of explanation has significant establishing power, it does not tell the entire story.

Some incumbents survive, some prosper, and some pioneer radical new technologies and dominate post-disruption market place. There is a considerable early research to suggest the ways to gauze responses due to incumbent's inflexibility or inertia, in the face of a disruptor's entry (Hill and Rothaermel, 2003) :

a) The performance of an incumbent firm will be higher if the firm's basic research function is loosely coupled with applied research functions. Loose coupling implies the development of mechanisms for coordination and integration between business units, as well as central research personnel some but not complete freedom, in their choice of research initiatives.

b) The performance of an incumbent firm will be higher, if the values and norms of firm legitimize autonomous and immediate response and action. The immediate and autonomous action is institutionalited through internal systems and procedures specifically designed to encourage and fund initiation as well as provide regular evaluation of new products and services.

c) The performance of an incumbent firm will be higher if the markets the firm serves have a history of turbulence that the firm has navigated in the past.

d) The longer the gestation period of that technological innovation, the higher the performance of an incumbent firm.

e) Use of strategic alliances to gain access to radical innovations pioneered by new entrants, thereby increasing the incumbent's post discontunity performance.

f) The performance of an incumbent firm will be higher if the firm has accumulated significant organizational slack from its established operations. Organizational slack is defined as the cushion or fund of actual or potential resources which allows an organization to adapt successfully to external resources for change in policy, as well as to initiate changes in strategy with respect to the external environment.

g) Incumbent firm will be in a better position if the firm possesses downstream complimentary assets that are critical to the commercialization of new technology.

h) There is an increasing returns aspect to knowledge accumulation with those that gain an early lead, are able to build on knowledge advantage, where as those that fail to invest in knowledge acquisition risk being locked out. So once an incumbent sleeps on the aspects of knowledge of a disruptor entry, may find it difficult to catch up.

The Necessity of Innovation

There is a wide acceptance in all industries arround the world about the increasing need of innovation. A survey by Strategos, a Gary Hamel consultancy firm, reveals that how the respondents feel about the importance of innovation figure 13. At the same time most companies feel that they are ill-equipped to foster innovation at the workplace. And they blame it on lack of effect iveness (fig. 14.a) and poor ideation (fig. 14.b).

Heavy incumbent satisfaction over present status tend to make them lethergic. The companies recognize that number of serious barriers stand in the way for effective innovation. Generally lacking in all organizations are the aggressiveness, and effort to understand the future. There is a tendency to dismiss innovation as something excessive and unscalable in business. Fig. 15 shows the status of barriers to innovation

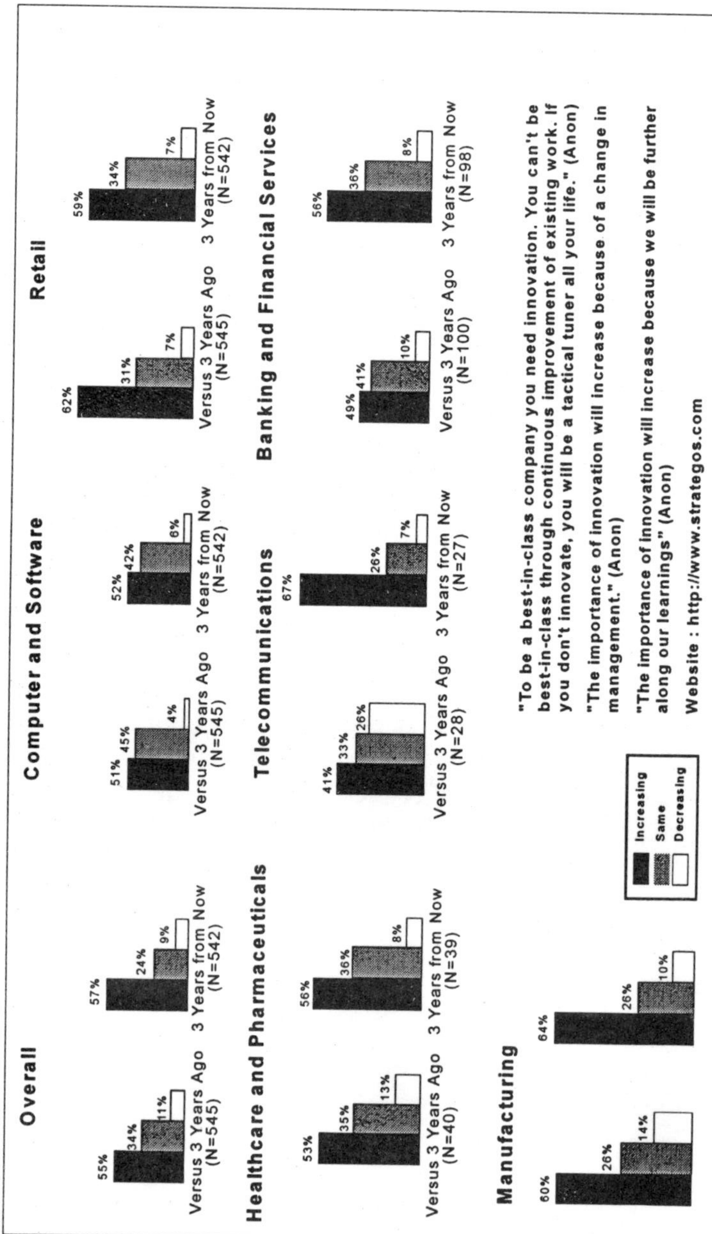

Fig. 13 The importance of innovation: Strategos' survey Computer and Software.

"People contrast investing in the base business, where they know the returns, land investing in new businesses where they don't - so they invest in what they know."

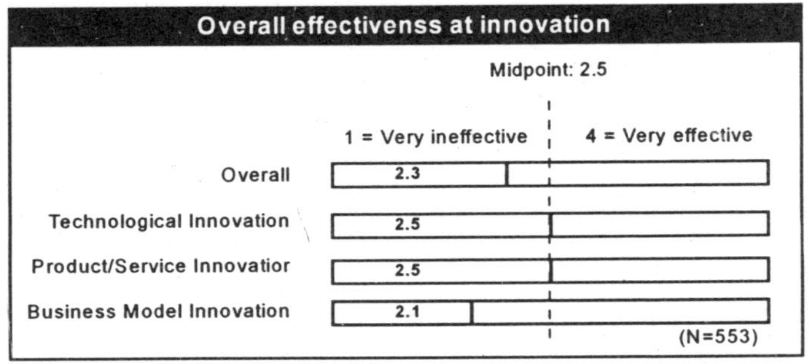

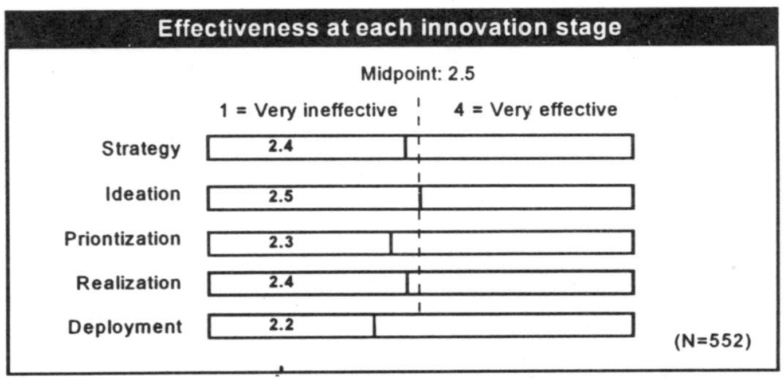

"Ideation is the weakest stage for us." (Anon)

"We are poor at execution, explaining the lowest rating given to deployment. (Anon)

(Courtesy : Strategos' survey '2004)

Fig. 14 Most companies rate themselves poorly at innovation.

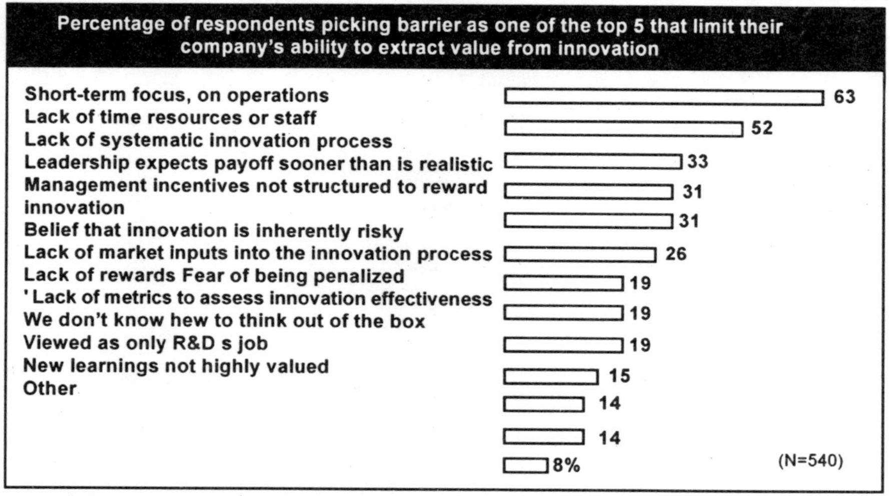

"There are lots of activities, ... but people lose interest no persistence or patience." (Anon)

"There is no clear accountability for innovation." (Anon)

"The mindset of the organization is very short-term, operationally-related. Every division has a P&L, and nothing gets done without a clear line of sight to return and shareholder value. Ideas go on the back burner or get dropped if they don't demonstrate an impact on the bottom-line in 3 years or less. "(Anon)

"Biggest barrier to success is balancing rigorous examination of ideas while not making people's notivation to keep coming with ideas" (Anon)

N : No. of respondents

(Courtesy : Strategos' survey '2004)

Website : http://www.strategos.com

Fig. 15 Serious barriers stand in the way of effective innovation.

Case Study - 12

The Game is never up! The upcoming marriage of fixed and mobile phones

An increasing number of people, are "cutting the cord" and going entirely mobile, doing away with their fixed lines altogether. And while fixed-line phones have many handy features, such as the ability to store dozens of names and numbers, not to mention text messaging and other services.

Fixed-line phones do have their advantages. Calls are cheaper and clearer, and connections are much more reliable, as anyone who has trouble getting a strong mobile signal indoors will testify. Hence the current enthusiasm throughout the telecoms industry for the idea of "fixed-mobile convergence", which uses clever technology to provide the best of both worlds: the freedom of mobile and the reliability and low cost of fixed lines. Subscribers use the same handset to make calls via fixed lines at home, and mobile networks when out and about: they have one number and one voicemail box, and receive one bill.

Behind the scenes, this involves some clever tricks. Calls are handled within the home by a small base-station plugged into a fixed-line broadband-internet connection. This base-station communicates with nearby handsets using radio technology that operates in "unlicensed" spectrum, such as Bluetooth or Wi-Fi (so you will need a new handset). The base-station pretends, in effect, to be an ordinary mobile-phone base-station. As you enter your house, your phone "roams" on to it. When you make a call, it is routed over the broadband link, which has enough capacity to handle several calls at once by different this way are billed as fixed-line calls. If you leave the house while making a call, you roam seamlessly back on to the ordinary mobile network. And when a friend comes to visit, her phone roams on to your base-station, but the charges for any calls made appear on her bill.

▸

Road mapping

For fixed-line operators such as BT (Britain's Telecoms) incumbent and one of the leading proponents of fixed-mobile convergence, the appeal of this approach is obvious: rather than losing out to mobile phones, fixed lines can now co-operate with them, and win back some traffic. After selling off its wireless arm a few-years ago, BT has reentered the mobile market by reselling airtime on other operators' networks; most recently, it has formed a partnership with Vodafone. A converged fixed-mobile service will enable BT to lower costs shifting some mobile calls on to its fixed network; it will also allow the company to differentiate itself from mobile-only operators.

Covergence

So-called integrated operators, which own both fixed and mobile networks-such as Germany's Deutsche Telekom and Japan's NTT-also like the idea of fixed-mobile convergence. They can save money by merging network infrastructures and doing away with separate fixed and mobile divisions. France Telecom, for example is reorganising itself into consumer and business divisions, rather than fixed and mobile. And Cingular, an American mobile operator owned by two fixed-line incumbents, BellSouth and SBC, is pursuing convergence as a way to improve coverage within buildings, and thus exploit fixed networks to gain a competitive advantage over other mobile operators.

Even mobile-only operators are getting involved, and making deals with fixed-line providers. Fixed-mobile convergence could help them fill the excess capacity on their 30 networks, and enable them to unload calls on to cheaper fixed networks where possible, to reduce costs. In short, everyone in the telecoms industry seems -to like the idea, because they hope it will expand the market overall. Once people get into the habit of carrying their mobile phones around with them at all times, even in the home, they will probably make more calls. Vendors love the idea too, notes David Brown of Motorola, the world's second-largest mobile-

▸

handset maker, because as well as requiring lots of back-did equipment, fixed-mobile convergence presents the opportunity to replace a billion or so existing fixed-line phones.

Alliance and standardization

It all sounds great, which explains why the idea of fixed-mobile convergence has been around for several years. But it is only now gaining any traction.

One reason, says Niel Ransom of Alcatel, a telecoms equipment maker, is important for the success of mobile phones: fixed-mobile convergence only makes sense if everyone has their own handset, which they now do, in the rich world at least. It is also now possible to cram multiple radios (one for mobile use, and one for use within buildings) into a single handset without adding much to its cost or size. But perhaps most important of all is the emergence of technical standards. This month a consortium of operators and suppliers, including Alcatel, BT, Cingular, Ericsson, Motorola, Nokia, Nortel and T-Mobile, announced specifications for integrating wide-area mobile with short-range Bluetooth and Wi-Fi networks. An agreed standard means that operators can proceed without the risk of beinglocked in to a particular technology.

Most observers agree that BT is the operator to watch. In July, 2004 it co-founded an alliance of operators called the Fixed Mobile Convergence Alliance, the other members of which include NTT, Brasil Telecom and Korea Telecom. BT's trailblazing fixed-mobile convergence technology, known as "Bluephone", is being developed by a seven-company consortium that includes Alcatel, Motorola and Ericsson, and is being closely watched by other operators.

The uncertainty

The big unanswered question is: do consumers actually want these new converged phone services? BT plans to market Bluephone or; the basis that it is a simplifying technology, yet explaining exactly how it simplifies things is not easy. "Education is needed, and a focus on simplicity,"

▶

says Andrew Cole of A.T. Kearney, a consultancy. One way to think of fixed-mobile convergence, he suggests, is that it brings the features of mobile phones into the fixed environment. Market research shows that people are receptive to the idea, he says, particularly if it means lower prices.

"If Bluephone proves a success in Britain, it is likely to trigger the launch of similar services elsewhere. Mobile-only operators may then rush to team up with cable operators in order to compete, since being a mobile-only or fixed-only operator will no longer be viable," says Lars Godell of Forrester, a consultancy. More companies might also follow the lead of France Telecom, arid merge their fixed and mobile divisions. If it all of this comes to pass, this will be yet another example, how incumbent can come back to reclaim the lost ground.

Research into the Role of Organizational Capability in Disruptive Success

A new research designed with a questionnaire survey by van Riel , Lemmink and Ouwersloot (2004) points to the following regarding organizational requirement to be able to succeed with innovation ,particularly in high technology services. The results though empirical provide some good insights:

	Study Hypotheses	**Test result**
1.	A positive relationship exists between the effort an organization puts into gathering intelligence with respect to developments in	1. Indirect success:
a.	Technology.	a. Partially supported.
b.	Competitors' strategies.	b. Rejected.
c.	Customer requirements, and the likelihood of innovation success in that organization.	c. Partially supported

2.	A positive relationship exists between the extent to which organization stimulates informal communication and the likelihood of innovation success in that organization	2. Indirect success: Partially supported
3.	A direct positive relationship exists between the extent to which the organization maintains an innovative climate and the likelihood of innovation success in that organization.	3. Indirect success: Supported
4.	A positive relationship exists between the extent to which the involved decision makers augment and update their knowledge proactively and the likelihood of innovation success.	4. Indirect success: Partially supported.

N.B: Indirect sucess refers to success otherwise achieved but not as such attempted.

Conclusions

The wisdom offered to the business community for over four decades is that for a business to maximize its economic value the business must be oriented totally to "finding contemporary needs and filling them" rather than to " make and selling them". This supported the now cliché but still very relevant dictum" business must be market oriented'. The proactive mechanism will be more successful than responsive mechanism. The strength of the pro-active market orientation relationship to the new product success would be more than that of responsive orientation, and as large if not more than that of merely innovation orientation.

Disruption has been and will continue to be a tremendous source of growth in the economy. It will also continue to attack established markets and destroy entrenched businesses. Managers who understand that the net effect of disruptive innovation is positive will be in a much better position to seek out new opportunities. They will build organizations that can identify promising new customers and stick with them as they pursue the innovation that leads to major new growth.

References

1. Ahuja. G. and Lampert. C. (2001) Enlrepreneurship in the Large Corporation: a longitudinal study of how established firms create breakthrough inventions. *Strategic Management Journal* 22, 52 1-543.
2. Astley. G.W. (1885) The two ecologies: Population and community perspectives on organisational evolution. *Administrative Science Quarterly* 224-241.
3. Baden-Fuller, C. and Pitt, M. (19%) *Strategic Innovation,* Routledge, London. Betz, F. (1993) *Strategic Technology Management.* McGraw-Hill, New York.
4. businesswire.com (2000) *Digital Disrupters Enables Companies to Thrive on Disruptive Innovation: Digital Disrupters (TM) Creates Groundbreaking B2B e-businesses in Unique Equity-Partnership Arrangements with Established Industry Leaders* (WWW document). Available at: http://www.businesswire.com/webbox/bw.040500/200961158.htm. Accessed 2001.
5. Bower J.L., "Teradyne: Managing Disruptive Change," Harvard Business School case no. 9-397-112 (Boston:Harvard Business School Publishing, 1997).
6. Christensen. C.M. and Rosenbloom, R. (1995) Explaining the attacker's advantage: technological paradigms, organisational dynamics and the value network. *Research Policy* 24, 233-257.
6. Christensen. C.M. , M.W. Johnson and D.K. Rigby, "Foundations for Growth: How To Identify and Build Disruptive New Businesses," MIT Sloan Management Review 43 (spring 2002): 22-31.
7. Christensen C.M. and G.C. Rogers, "Hewlett Packard: The Flight of the Kittyhawk," Harvard Business School case no. 9-697-060 (Boston: Harvard Business School Publishing, 1997).

8. Christensen, C.M. (1997) *The Innovators Dilemma: when new technologies cause great firms to fail.* Harvard Business School Press. Boston. Massachusetts.
9. Day. G. and Schoemaker. P. (Oct 9, 2000) Don't Hesitate to Innovate. *Financial Times* Survey - Mastering Management edn. 6 The Financial Times Ltd. Hard Copy on File, Soft copy in z:/references/financial times (2000). Survey - Mastering Management.
10. Dosi, G. (1982) Technological paradigms and technological trajectories. *Research Policy* 147-162.
11. Anon (2004), The Marriage of two phones" The Economistry 25th Sept., 71-72
12. Eisenmann T.R. , "Internet Business Models: Text and Cases" (New York: McGraw Hill, 2002).
13. Gilbert. C. and J.L. Bower, "Disruptive Change: When Trying Harder Is Part of the Problem," Harvard Business Review 80 (May 2002): 94-101.
14. Hamel, G. (2000) *Leading the Revolution,* Harvard Business School Press. Boston. Massachusetts.
15. Hamel G. and Getz G (2004), "Funding growth in an age of austerity," Harvard Business Rerview, July-Aug, 76-84
16. Hill C.W.L. and Rothaermel (2003), "The Performance of incumbent firms in the face of radical technological innovation" Academy of Management Review, Vol 28, No.2., 257 - 274.
17. Hill. C.W.L. and Jones. G.R. (1998) *Strategic Management: An Integrated Approach,* Houghton Mifflin Company. Boston. NY.
18. Johnson. G. and Scholes. K. (1997) *Exploring Corporate Strategy,* Prentice Hall. London.
19. Moore. G.A. (1995) *Inside the Tornado: Marketing Strategies from Silicon Valley's Cutting Edge,* HarperCollins, New York.
20. Overdorf. M. (2000) Meeting the Challenge of Disruptive Innovation. *Harvard Business Review* March/April, 69
21. Manjari Raman (2004) "Can Infosys be a disruptive innovator, the strategist, Business & Standard, Jan 20.

22. Rice. M.P., Kelly. D., Peters. L., O'Connor and Gina Colarelli (2001) Radical Innovation: triggering initiation of opportunity recognition and evaluation. *R& I) Management,* 31 (4). 409-420.

23. Schumpeter. J.A. (1942) *Capitalism, Socialism and Democracy.* Harper & Row (originally published in 1942 by Harper and Brothers), New York.

24. Schumpeter, J.A. (1934) , "The theory of economic development," cambridge, MA : Harvard University Press

25. Tidd, J., Bessant, J. and Pavvit. K. (1997) *Managing Innovation: Integrating technological, market and organizational change,* John Wiley & Sons Ltd., Chichester.

26. Trott, P. (1998) Innovation Management & New Product Development. Pearson Education, Harlow.

27. Trott, P. (2001) The role of market research in the development of discontinuous new products. European Journal of Innovation Management 4. I 17-125.

28. Tushman. M.L. and Anderson, P. (1986) Technological discontinuities and organizational environments. Administrative Science Quarterly 31.439-465.

29. Unsworth. K. (2001) Unpacking creativity. Academy of Management Review 26. 289-297.

30. Van riel, Lemmink and Ouwersloodt (2004)," High – Technology Service Innovation Success: A Decision Making Perspective", Journal of Product Innovation Management, vol 21, No.5, p 348-359.

31. Veryzer. R.W. (1998) Discontinuous Innovation and the New Product Development Process. Journal of Product Innovation Management, (15). 304-321.

32. Walsh, S.T. (2004). Roadmapping a Disruptive Technology: A Cash study. The Emerging Microsystems and top-down nanosystems industry" Technology Forecasting and Social Change, vol 71, page. 161-185."

33. Vojak B and Chambers F (2004), "Roadmapping Disruptive technical threats and opportunities in complex technology based subsystems: The SAILS methodology" Technology forecasting and Social change, vol 71, p 121-139.